It's Good to be *Queen*

Every Woman's Pocket Guide to Financial Sovereignty

ROSELYN WILKINSON, MBA, CFP®

It's Good to be Queen: Every Woman's Pocket Guide to Financial Sovereignty
© 2018
By Roselyn Wilkinson, MBA, CFP®

Roselyn Wilkinson is a registered representative and investment advisory associate of Berthel Fisher & Company Financial Services, Inc. The views and opinions expressed are those of the registered representative and do not necessarily reflect those of Berthel Fisher & Company Financial Services, Inc. or any regulatory body. Neither the information nor any opinion expressed constitutes a solicitation by the representative for the purchase of any securities or any particular investment. It does not constitute an offer nor a solicitation to sell products or services or engage in investment related activities of any kind.

ISBN-13: 978-1986872300
ISBN-10: 1986872300

Cover Design: Lee Ann Fortunato-Heltzel and Anne Hussman
Editor: Gina Mazza (ginamazza.com)
Interior Layout: Lee Ann Fortunato-Heltzel (creativeonemarketing.com)

Roselyn Wilkinson
Pittsburgh, PA
www.Good2BQueen.com
roselynw@good2bqueen.com

10 9 8 7 6 5 4 3 2 1

Dedication

To Chip, Ryan, Joseph, Ellie and John,
my tireless cheerleaders.

Praise for
Roselyn Wilkinson and

It's Good
to be
Queen

This highly practical and informative book is written with a clear and friendly voice, making an otherwise daunting topic easy and accessible.
   –Linda Babcock, PhD
   James M. Walton Professor of Economics at
   Carnegie Mellon University
   Co-author of *Women Don't Ask: The High
   Cost of Avoiding Negotiation—and Positive
   Strategies for Change*

An enjoyable and empowering read for women of any age at any stage. Wilkinson carefully explains the financial basics in enough detail to be helpful but without tedium and intimidating jargon. It's what every woman needs to take control of her finances and her life.
   –Heather Arnet
   CEO, Women & Girls Foundation

The author's passion to eliminate the time worn "princess message" and instead empower girls and women shines through each page. She makes it simple and fun to take responsibility for one's financial health. Fathers of girls, you need to read this book too!
   –Aradhna Malhotra Oliphant
   President and CEO,
   Leadership Pittsburgh, Inc.

This book speaks to me as a professional, mother and advocate. Wilkinson artfully guides the reader to fearlessly take charge of her own "happily ever after." Her tips and tools help women understand and navigate key financial decisions throughout their lives. A must read for women of all ages, educators and those who wish to change the current narrative.

—Jennifer Cairns, Esq.
Executive Director, Sarah Heinz House

If your eyes glaze over when it comes to your money, this book is for you. Wilkinson's inventive approach will give you the courage to build financial literacy like a queen. With her straightforward advice, you need not resort to the damsel-in-distress approach, avoiding what you don't understand and hoping to be rescued.

—Tracy Fuller
Executive Director, Compio
Author of *Lifelong Leadership:
A Personal Sourcebook*

This inspiring book gives women what they need to take control of their financial futures. It covers a remarkable amount of financial information in an easily understandable manner. Read it then get one (or more) for the women you love.

—Richard Citrin, PhD, MBA
Citrin Consulting

Contents

Introduction

*"I'm not a princess. I don't need saving.
I'm a queen. I've got this shit handled."*
— Anonymous

It's considered a "timeless classic." You know the story, the kind your parents read to you at bedtime when you were a little girl. The plot is some version of this:

Through no fault of her own, a young maiden is mistreated and finds herself at the mercy of a wicked queen or other scoundrel. She faces horrible trials and horrendous tribulations until, low and behold, she is rescued at the eleventh hour by Prince Charming. From that moment on — sometimes all it takes is a kiss or a recovered glass slipper — she lives happily ever after, ne'er to be in distress again.

Fairy tales have their place in sparking the imaginations of young girls, but they're not real. When it comes to women living in the modern era with a sense of financial security, this folklore rendition of life can be misleading, even downright disastrous. My guess is that you don't buy into these myths hook, line and sinker, either. You want to feel empowered about your financial security, or else you wouldn't be reading this book. As a financial advisor for more than 25 years, I've found that many women abdicate their financial planning to almost any man in their lives — their husbands, fathers and, perhaps worst of all, their son's college roommate who is just getting started in the investment business.

I'd like to help change all of that, and update the fairy tale to a current day classic in which women feel as vested in their financial lives as they do in other parts of their lives, such as their career and health. Handing this power over to someone else, no matter how charming, doesn't necessarily lead to a happy ending. The truth is, nobody's going to care about your money more than you do, and no one else is going to have to rely on it for the long term as you will.

I'd like to suggest that it's even more important for women than men to have a firm handle on their financial picture. Why? Because women face unique challenges that most men don't.[1] They:

- have longer life expectancies.
- earn less income and, no surprise, have less savings.[2,3]
- are more likely to take career breaks for caregiving of children, parents or other family members.
- have less confidence when it comes to investing and as a result often invest too conservatively.[4]

For these reasons and more, women would be wise to make thoughtful, informed decisions about their financial security both in the short and long run. Owning your financial success is one of the best ways to preserve your independence and expand your options in life. And if you do meet that special someone, you can decide whether to share the wealth or not.

As you read through these pages, I'd like you to bear a few things in mind. First, don't get lost in the numbers. Investments and financial planning can involve very sophisticated projections, but as I will demonstrate, it's no more complicated than eighth-grade math. If you can add, subtract, multiply, divide and figure percentages, you've got this.

Second, be aware (and simply accept) that the financial industry has its own vocabulary, just like the legal, medical and many other professions. It's a language, though, that can be learned in order to have a working knowledge of it. All that's required is taking time to understand what each term means. To make it easier to grasp and quicker to locate and master this terminology, I've highlighted certain words and phrases

....

[1] US Department of Health and Human Services, *Chartbook on Long-Term Trends in Health* (2016) 14-15.

[2] US Department of Labor Statistics *Women in the Labor Force: A Databook* (December 2015).

[3] 17th Annual Transamerica Retirement Survey (December 2016) 152-156.

[4] Croson, Rachel and Gneezy, Uri, "Gender Differences in Preferences," *Journal of Economic Literature*, (June 2009) 7.

throughout the chapters; the Appendix also includes a glossary of commonly used financial industry terms.

Third, as you dive into this material, begin with the end in mind. A common question that I will ask throughout the chapters is: "What are your goals?" Once you know where you're going, together we can construct strategies to get you there. Your goals might change over time and that's okay, too.

Fourth, in each chapter you'll find a Once Upon A Time tale based on my years of working with clients. The names have been changed to protect the innocent (and guilty). Far from fairy tales, these are real life examples that you can learn from. The Keys to the Castle bullet points serve as takeaways from the chapters' lessons.

As you step forward with your royal robe and scepter in hand, I will lead you through the main components of taking control of your financial life, including how to budget, stay out of debt, plan for the future, protect and save your assets, and more. Should you choose to seek professional help with your investment and retirement decisions, the book covers what you need to know about finding and vetting qualified professionals. I have included resources and worksheets in the Appendix so that you can learn more.

Before we begin, allow me to dispel one more myth. Money does not buy happiness. That's more about having what you want and wanting what you have. It does, however, buy you options. Regardless of whether you're single, married, divorced or widowed, it's best to begin managing your money strategically as soon as possible because the older you get, the more important having choices and possibilities becomes.

If the topic of finances makes you feel overwhelmed, you've come to the right place. That's why I wrote this guidebook. By the time you're done reading these chapters, you'll have everything you need to write your own financial story. Because today, happily ever after is not a fairy tale; it's a choice.

Part One

The Timeworn Fairy Tale:
Waiting For a Knight
in Shining Armor

One
Damsel in Distress No More

"I think part of being an adult is leaving the fairy tale behind."
—Rashida Jones, film/TV actor, comic book author,
screenwriter and singer

Snow White's fairer than the queen. Rapunzel is cursed with selfish old Mother Gothel. Cinderella has a wicked stepmother.[5] Damsels in distress are everywhere and have been a part of storytelling folklore since as far back as the time of ancient Greece and India. From the 17th through the 19th Centuries, the Brothers Grimm, Charles Perrault and Hans Christian Anderson were big fans of this plot line, which set up female characters needing to be rescued by charming princes. In recent decades, women fairy tale protagonists have fared better. The Little Mermaid isn't pitted against an evil queen. Instead, Arielle rescues the prince — but at what cost? She gives up her voice in hope of marrying him.

Alas, these fairy tales are fictional accounts of epic life experiences written to entertain us, yet they pervade our culture with a message of feminine vulnerability. It starts by reading these stories to young children – mostly little girls,[6] but little boys, too. It has also been perpetuated in

....

[5] Sometimes an older woman is pitted against a young beautiful woman. That's another subliminal message we need to examine, but is a subject for a whole other book.

[6] For alternative good night stories, see *Good Night Stories for Rebel Girls: 100 Tales of Extraordinary Women* by Elena Favilli and Francesca Cavallo, Timbuktu Labs, Inc. (2016).

books and movies into the 20th and 21st Centuries. On the silver screen, *Pretty Woman,* with Julia Roberts and Richard Gere, was the ultimate fairy tale of a beautiful prostitute and billionaire businessman who fall in love. Since its debut in 1990, it has grossed more than $460 million worldwide. The HBO television series *Sex & the City* aired for 10 years and spawned two feature films. While the series broke new ground with the theme of independent women who spoke freely of sex, career and other conquests, three of the four main characters, all in their thirties, were largely in pursuit of their own Prince Charming. Even when the main character, the beloved sex columnist and fun fashionista Carrie Bradshaw, falls hopelessly in love with Mr. Big, the rich businessman, he is unwilling to commit to her.

Children model what they see, even if it's fictional in nature. Classic fairy tales and their modern interpretations lead readers and viewers to believe, even if subconsciously, that their futures lie in factors completely beyond their control, and that females need "saving." (I'm all for saving, just not in that way.)

The damsel-in-distress model doesn't just do a disservice to our daughters; it's not helping our sons either. Why should they be burdened with rescuing their partners when more than half of couples today have both partners working outside the home?[7] Let's hold onto the other princely attributes of virtue, manners and fashion sense, but chuck the rest. In other words, let's take a few of the best-known tales and mix them up a bit so they better reflect our current reality.

The classic version of *Cinderella* tells us that her father remarries and her stepmother banishes her to cleaning the house and sleeping by the fireplace. A combination of circumstances gets her to the ball and she dances with the prince for a few hours, falling head over heels in love. Our dear Cindy rushes to leave by the stroke of midnight, losing one of her glass slippers. You know the rest.

Now, what if Cindy could instead turn her plight into a career opportunity? She might decide to leverage her familiarity with fireplaces into a job as a chimney sweep, a traditionally male occupation. Maybe

---

[7] US Bureau of Labor Statistics, *Women in the Labor Force: A Databook* (December 2015).

she gets so good at it that her reputation builds throughout the land and she ends up having more chimneys to clean than she can handle. So, she starts enlisting help and a woman-owned business is born. Her sales territory is dense since every homeowner in the land has at least 2.5 fireplaces. Eventually, she expands into disaster restoration for homes and businesses damaged by fire, even producing her own line of fireplace tools made from the local forge — with brass pumpkin finials, no less.

How about the tale of poor little Snow White? She is exiled to the forest by her jealous stepmother and comes to live with seven dwarves with funny names. Maybe she's not so poor after all. Given her work with the little guys, her managerial expertise grows. A useful skill set, Ms. White parlays her team-building competencies into a position at the local mine where her buddies dig, dig, dig, all day long. Next thing you know – heigh ho – she advances to a leadership position dealing with all personality types like Grumpy, Sleepy, Dopey and Bashful. Snowy ends up working with the HR Department to help the mine company start a retirement plan for all of its employees to save, save, save, all day long.

Oh, I don't know what you've been told
But this gal right here's gonna rule the world

Then Snow White / She did it right /In her life
Had seven men to do the chores /
'Cause that's not what a lady's for

"Sit Still, Look Pretty" performed by Daya
Gino Maurice Barletta / Scott Bruzenak / Mike Campbell / Britten Newbill
Kobalt Music Publishing Ltd., 2015

Sleeping Beauty would no doubt have more opportunity in today's world, too. As you'll probably recall, Aurora's story began with a witch's curse that her untimely demise would come from pricking her finger on a spindle. Although her father banishes all spindles from his kingdom, she discovers one while exploring her castle. Well, we wouldn't have a story if she didn't prick her finger on that lone spindle and fall asleep for 100 years before the prince ambles by to rescue her. What if instead Aurora parlays that spinning wheel into a career in textile manufacturing or fashion design, perhaps foreshadowing Anne Klein or Donna Karan? Maybe engineering is her calling and her finger-pricking experience inspires her to invent a safer sewing machine.

Over in the tower, Rapunzel's knack for magic hair might lead her to become a successful stylist and manage a franchise network of Golden Hair salons. Our little mermaid Arielle's commitment to search and rescue could lead her to a career with the Coast Guard. The Princess and the Pea? Yes, she goes into sales for a memory foam mattress company, as she can empathize with how important it is for people to get a good night's sleep.

You get the picture. So, the question is: Why do we keep teaching girls to be princesses anyway? Isn't there something better to aspire to? Yes, there is. If we're going to spin fantasies about royalty, wouldn't it be more appropriate to skip the princess and step right up to queen? After all, the queen rules, right? She's got the power, the crown jewels and the real estate. In fact, have you noticed that being queen is such a great gig that they never quit their jobs? Queen Elizabeth II has held the throne for more than 60 years. Not only is she the queen of England, she's also technically the queen of Australia, Canada and several island nations.

When the movie *Frozen* came along in 2014, it was a breath of fresh air and wildly received by kids and parents alike. Fundamentally, it is a story of the strong and enduring love between two sisters. There is a Prince Charming but he turns out to be an insincere jerk plotting against both sisters to overtake their family's kingdom. Our protagonist, Princess Anna, is strong and independent. Queen Elsa is a commanding female, but must leave the island due to uncontrolled ice powers. So, we're making progress but still vilifying the queen in our modern fairy tales. And the classics die hard. Case in point: *Cinderella* was made into a live action film as recently as 2015, *Sleeping Beauty* has been turned into a movie seven times, and *Snow White* has had 20 iterations since 1900.

All of this is subtly changing, though. In recent years, a groundswell has been building within our culture to banish the princess message. Google "anti-princess movement" and you'll see what I mean. This book hopes to be part of that sea change, but it's not going away without a fight. The "Disney princess" brand generates billions of dollars marketing across multimedia, spreading the message through movies, games, videos, activities and theme parks all over the world. There is so much money involved that in 2013, the US Patent Office issued a trademark to Disney Enterprises, Inc. for the name "Snow White" that covers all live and recorded movie, television, radio, stage, computer,

Internet, news and photographic entertainment uses. Between their costumes and action figures, they want children to play with them and as them. And this marketing isn't geared just towards children. Disney has partnered with Zales Jewelers on their "Happily Forever After" Enchanted Disney fine jewelry collection, replete with TV commercials of princess silhouettes and an online quiz for women to determine which type of princess they are.

The princess message spreads beyond books, movies and advertising. Pittsburgh, where I live, is host to the second-oldest

Cinderella Ball in the United States. Do we need debutantes in 2018? Debatable, but can we at least call it something other than the Cinderella Ball? The young women who take part in this coming-of-age ritual deserve recognition for the volunteer work that they do in their communities (a prerequisite for participating in the ball) and, yes, there's a scholarship to be had, which sweetens the pot. The event raises thousands of dollars for charities around the city. I'm good with all of that, but here's where I take issue: At the end of said ball, a "Prince Charming" selects his "Cinderella" by choosing one of the debutantes' names out of a pumpkin.[8] Really?

It's beyond time to encourage a fresh narrative on women, so let's take a quick reality check about the influence and power that women actually have in the 21st Century. One recent study by UBS Wealth Management reveals how couples think about money[9]:

- 50% responded that a man's responsibility is investing, insurance, long-term planning and bill paying.
- 37% equally divided responsibility for real estate, other large purchases, estate planning and college funding.
- 13% responded that a woman's responsibility is bill paying, day-to-day expenses and charitable donations.

It's not uncommon for the female in a traditional relationship to control the checkbook and pay the daily expenses. As the primary caregivers for children and the elderly, women buy on behalf of themselves and their extended families.[10] Women drive 70% to 80% of all consumer purchases through a combination of buying power and influence, with total purchasing power of at least $5 trillion annually. All of this makes them prime candidates for ruling over their own financial queendom. So let's get started!

---

[8] www.cinderellaball.com

[9] "Couples and Money: Who Decides," *UBS Investor Watch: Analyzing Investor Sentiment and Behavior* (2Q 2014).

[10] Brennan, Bridget, "Top 10 Things Everyone Should Know About Women Consumers," *Forbes Magazine* (January 21, 2015).

"The wolf said, "You know, my dear, it isn't safe for a little girl to walk through these woods alone." Red Riding Hood said, "I find your sexist remark offensive in the extreme, but I will ignore it because of your traditional status as an outcast from society, the stress of which has caused you to develop your own, entirely valid, worldview. Now, if you'll excuse me, I must be on my way."

—James Finn Garner, *Politically Correct Bedtime Stories*

Two

Happily Ever After as Ms., Miss or Mrs.

Let's get this straight right up front. Today, women control 51%, or $14 trillion, of the personal wealth in the United States and are anticipated to control $22 trillion by 2020.[11] Yet only about 8% of women feel knowledgeable about managing investments[12] and many worry about becoming the proverbial "bag lady" in old age. Even women who earn more than $200,000 a year have this fear.[13] It's a legitimate concern. The National Institute on Retirement Security, a nonprofit research center, reports that women are 80% more likely than men to be impoverished at age 65 and older. Women age 75 to 79 are three times more likely.

Why is that? How does this happen? It has something to do with that tricky concept of "happily ever after." As the story goes, you must kiss quite a few frogs to find and marry your supposed prince. When you do find Mr. Right, there's no guarantee that the marriage will last

---

[11] "Despite Controlling $14 Trillion in Wealth, American Women Still Have Challenges to Overcome," BMO Financial Group (April 2, 2015).

[12] "What Really Matters to Women Investors," Russell Investments white paper (January 2014) 8.

[13] "Women Today: New Roles, New Responsibilities and New Financial Needs," Allianz white paper (2012) 7.

'til the end of time. In fact, the numbers seem to be working against women, when you consider that now fewer women are married than the combined total number of women who are single and divorced. If there's a silver lining here, it's that – despite conventional wisdom – the divorce rate is not rising and it is not true that half of all marriages end in divorce. The statistic is closer to 30%.[14] Not great, but better than 50%.

The fairy tales never mention how important it is that you and your mate think about money the same way, but this is very important. If one is a saver and the other a **spendthrift,** there may be trouble in paradise. You can imagine the dialogue: "You spend too much money" countered with "No, you don't make enough money." In fact, money is the number one topic that couples argue about. Obviously, the decision to marry and possibly co-mingle finances has a huge impact on your long-term financial situation. Yes, marriage is about love but it's also a contract that affects your financial stability, sometimes in ways that you can't foresee.

Few people get married preparing for divorce. But people change – many times for the better, but not always. You may be the one who wants out of the marriage, and you may not want to get back into another marriage. Although 60% of divorced and widowed individuals are likely to get remarried, 40% aren't.[15] Regardless of how a marriage ends, the breakup is typically more financially devastating to women than men. A woman's per capita household income drops as much as 15% and women have higher poverty rates, according to Nicholas Wolfinger, sociology professor at the University of Utah.

Even if you are in a happy relationship, there is no reason not to build your financial independence. Sometimes things go awry. Bad things happen. People die. You don't want to be a widow at all – let alone a widow-without-a-clue wondering where the money is.

---

[14] Miller, Claire Cain, "The Divorce Surge Is Over, but the Myth Lives On," *The New York Times* (December 2, 2014).

[15] Livingston, Gretchen, "Four-in-Ten Couples are Saying 'I Do' Again," Pew Social Trends (November 14, 2014).

I understand that women relinquishing control of their financial future is not always a conscious decision. On the other hand, many times it is. As a financial advisor, I've been amazed at the number of women who rely on the men in their lives to make their financial decisions. For single women, it's often their fathers. For widows, it might be a brother or brother-in-law. For couples, it often comes down to strictly a division of household labor – a time management strategy. Whether it's a traditional marriage with a stay-at-home spouse or one in which both partners work outside the home, there's a lot to be done to keep a household running, and divvying up the tasks can be an efficient way of getting things done.[16]

....

©Glasbergen
GLASBERGEN

"Compared to being eaten by a dragon or turned into a toad, I guess this counts as happily ever after."

I get it. You're busy and if you feel uneducated about the subject, it's easy to defer to someone who seems confident. Just because you've charged someone else (like your dad or your spouse) with this

---

[16] Bureau of Labor Statistics, American Time Use Survey news release (June 27, 2017).

responsibility doesn't necessarily mean this person is doing the best job at it. In fact, two-thirds of women state that they cannot rely on a spouse to handle the investing.[17] What if your partner says he's taking care of this but he's not – or, at least, not as well as it could be handled? What if he's lost in the woods without breadcrumbs and too embarrassed to ask for directions? Consider this: According to the **FINRA** Investor Education Foundation – a great resource – the percentage of Americans who can pass its five-question financial literacy test is just 37%. Despite this dismal score, 76% of the study participants (both men and women) gave themselves a "very high" rating on financial knowledge.[18] (Curious to take this test? I've put it in the Appendix and I recommend you take it *after* you've read this book.)

Even if your spouse is the designated family financial manager, there's no reason why you shouldn't stay involved in the process. Sure, you might get pushback from family members for taking an interest in the topic. Some might accuse you of not trusting your dad, son or brother to make appropriate decisions on your behalf. In response, just say that it's not a matter of trust but rather the three "E's" that come from being engaged in your own financial security: education, enjoyment and empowerment. If you're single, it's just not practical to rely on anyone else. No one is going to be with you the rest of your life like you will.

Or maybe the resistance might come directly from your partner. If so, support your position with the following thoughts:
- If you are planning to be together for the long term (which is the plan, right?), it's important that you are both committed to the same goals and strategies to reach them.
- You don't want to burden your partner with all the stress that comes from handling such a big responsibility.
- Two heads are better than one. In fact, men and women have been found to have complementary skills, especially when it comes to retirement planning, with men focusing on the revenue side of the

---

[17] "Women Today: New Roles, New Responsibilities and New Financial Needs," Allianz white paper (2012) 3.

[18] "Financial Capability in the United States," FINRA Investor Education Foundation (2015) 31.

equation and women on the expenses.[19]

By way of comparison, let's consider another important aspect of your life: your physical health. You wouldn't (or shouldn't) turn over control of your medical decisions to someone else. You probably wouldn't say to someone else, no matter how much you love them, "Hey, find me a doctor and make me an appointment. I'll go to that appointment but, whatever the diagnosis, you figure out my treatment plan and what medications I should take. Oh, and you decide what procedures I should have, too." Sounds ridiculous, right? It's just as crazy to take this approach with your financial health. Of course, you want their opinion and you undoubtedly want their support, but you wouldn't relinquish all decision-making. The same is true for your financial health.

ONCE UPON A TIME: CORRINE

Corrine's busy. Being a full-time stay-at-home mom is a big job. In fact, she barely sits down most days. Her husband, Kyle, is a lawyer in the early years of his career. It is not unusual for him to work 70 to 80 hours a week. Because he works all the time, Corrine handles everything else in their lives, including grocery shopping, cooking, laundry, doctor and dentist appointments. Of course, she also manages all the children's activities, like getting them to school, soccer practices and dance classes, as well as overseeing homework, getting them to bed on time and everything else.

When Kyle said he'd handle their investment decisions, Corrine was happy to have one less thing to do. She figured she'd get more involved in their finances when the kids are older and she has more time. Sounds like a plan, right? Well, I'm sad to say that her dear Kyle died of a heart

[19] Secure Retirement Planning Institute, LIMRA study (2016) as cited on www.foxbusiness.com, "Financial Decisions: Men vs. Women" (May 31, 2016).

attack at age 45 when their kids were still 'tweens. Corrine was completely in the dark about their finances and she was scared.

There is good news. Kyle had life insurance, and all those years he worked so hard led to him being a partner in his law firm. Upon his passing, the firm paid Corrine for his share of ownership in it. She also had the support of Kyle's family to help her manage the effects of Kyle's passing. The not-so-good news is that Kyle's brothers wanted to "take care of Corrine." They felt they knew best as far as managing the life insurance death benefits and the proceeds from the business. Grieving Kyle's loss and feeling overwhelmed and uneducated on their financial situation, Corrine was happy to let the brothers tell her what to do. Unfortunately, this left Corrine back in the same situation as when Kyle was alive: relying on someone else to make her financial decisions.

KEYS TO THE CASTLE:

- Don't abdicate your financial health to anyone else. Regardless of your marital status, be engaged in the decision making around your financial security.

- Even if you get resistance from your partner or family members, stay strong in your resolve to be a full participant in the financial decisions within your household.

Modern Day Royalty:Nobility Through Work and Career

Most women work outside the castle . . . er, home these days. Today, women comprise 20 to 25% of leadership positions in academia, law firms, the federal courts and the US Congress.[20] In the corporate world, lots of women are filling the pipeline, ready to move into the C-suite. We currently make up nearly 40% of MBA graduates and 40% of managers.[21] Recent surveys have found that firms with more women throughout the corporate structure are more profitable and record better stock market returns.[22] Unfortunately, less than 5% of *Fortune 500* CEOs are women and only one woman per year joins that exclusive group.[23]

There is still progress to be made in crashing through the glass ceiling. Women still bring home less money than men on average for the

[20] US Department of Labor Statistics, *Women in the Labor Force: A Databook* (December 2015).

[21] Marcus, Noland and Morgan, Tyler, "Study: Firms With More Women in the C-Suite Are More Profitable," *Harvard Business Review* (February 8, 2016).

[22] Salop, Kate R., "The One Thing That Will Get More Women in the C-Suite," *Fortune Magazine* (March 8, 2016).

[23] Marcus, Noland and Morgan, Tyler, "Study: Firms with More Women in the C-Suite Are More Profitable," *Harvard Business Review* (February 8, 2016).

same work (83 cents for every male-earned dollar).[24] At the same time, women pay more for goods and services than men and outlive them by an average of five years.[25] Several studies show that many items are routinely more expensive for women than for men. One study of 800 nearly identical products with male and female versions found that the women's products, on average, cost 7% more than the men's products.[26] Girl's clothing cost 4% more than boy's. Girl's toys are pricier, too: a red scooter costs $25 while a pink scooter has a $50 price tag, despite them being identical in all other ways. Women's clothing costs 8% more than men's, and women's personal care items cost 13% more.

You can think of this as a tax that women pay just because we're women. And a study from the state of California on this so-called **pink tax** found that women, on average, pay about $1,351 annually in extra costs for similar goods and services. This is true for everyday expenses like dry cleaning, as well as big-ticket items like cars and mortgages.

Although the equal-pay-for-equal-work battle continues, the good news is that women are earning more than ever. Today, 57% of women say that they have more earning power than ever before. About 40% are the primary breadwinners in their households and another 22% are co-breadwinners.[27] Not surprisingly, the higher the percentage of total income women bring into the household, the more sway they hold and the more engaged they are in the investing decisions. At the same time, many married women believe that making more money than their spouse could cause tension in the relationship.[28]

Statistics *also* show that women want to feel in control of their finances. A Wells Fargo survey of affluent women found that 90% enjoy making money and watching it grow. Two-thirds of these women said

[24] US Department of Labor Statistics, *Women in the Labor Force: A Databook* (December 2015).

[25] US Department of Health and Human Services, Centers for Disease Control and Prevention, National Center for *Health Statistics, Health: United States 2016: With Chartbook on Long-term Trends in Health*, 16.

[26] New York City Department of Consumer Affairs, *From Cradle to Cane: The Cost of Being a Female Consumer* (December 2015).

[27] Glynn, Sarah Jane, "Breadwinning Mothers Are Increasingly the US Norm," Center for American Progress (December 19, 2016).

[28] Regnier, Pat and Amanda Gengler, "Men, Women…and Money," www.CNNMoney.com (March 14, 2006).

they'd accumulated most of their wealth through investments and the stock market — yet just 46% are responsible for choosing and managing their household's investment accounts. Among married women, that number dips to 34%.[29] This is not ideal but it is understandable. Whether working outside the home or not, women still provide most of the elder care and childcare, so really, who has the time?

....

©Glasbergen

"Cinderella, I'm going to rescue you by turning that pumpkin into a coach — a success coach!"

When the Heir Apparent Arrives: Integrating Work and Family
Although the dialogue is changing such that "maternity" leave has expanded to "family" leave, it's still typically the woman whose financial picture changes when children arrive. If the couple can afford to subsist

....

[29] "Wells Fargo Survey: Affluent Women 'Enjoy' Making Money," www.Wellfargo.com (November 20, 2014).

on one partner's income, many women quit working outside the castle completely when they start a family. The rationale is that child daycare costs could exceed what they would earn in their careers, but is this the best financial strategy? I believe it is a flawed calculation for the following reasons[30]:

1. It is short sighted. A woman's current salary is not her future salary. If she continues to work outside the home, she will progress in her career and keep current with technology, her skill set will expand and her earnings will increase.

2. In this scenario, the childcare expenses are counted only against the woman's income instead of as a family expense, for which both parents are responsible. Since all income contributes to the family's expenses while she is working outside the home, all income should contribute to the family's expenses when she's not.

3. Although we don't typically think of it as such, continuing to work outside the home can serve as a kind of insurance, too. (We'll get into this in more detail in Chapter 6.)

ONCE UPON A TIME: BETSY

Betsy and Bill have been married 20 years. When they started a family, they decided that Betsy would stay at home with the children. Bill continued to climb the corporate career ladder with his income steadily increasing. It wasn't long before he was making as much on his salary as he and Betsy did together when she was still working outside the home. Not only did Bill survive several layoffs at his firm, he eventually made vice president; next was executive vice president and all was well. Bill and Betsy bought a bigger castle. Their kids wanted for nothing and their futures looked bright, too, as

---

[30] Mccolis, Jerry A. and Goodman, Marina, "Advising Married Women on Investing – In Themselves," *Journal of Financial Planning* (March 2014) 26-27.

Bill and Betsy funded their children's college savings accounts. The family travelled near and far, all about the land.

Then things took a turn for the worse. Bill's firm was bought by a larger company and they didn't need any more vice presidents. As the firm was "right-sized", Bill found himself needing outplacement counseling and undertaking a job search in his early fifties. Bill did not plan on this; neither had Betsy. They needed to adjust the lifestyle to which they had become accustomed . . . and fast. That meant Betsy going to work outside the home while Bill secured another position, which took a while. Thankfully, the children were self-sufficient at this point, so Betsy felt comfortable being gone when they got home from school most days. Bill shared with Betsy what he was learning through his outplacement counseling to help translate her home management and volunteering expertise to skills applicable in the world of paid employment. It wasn't easy. Betsy had been out of the workforce for a few decades and a lot of technology had passed her by. As a woman in her fifties, she also faced ageism with potential employers asking her questions like, "Aren't you getting close to retirement?" and "How much longer do you plan to work?"

KEYS TO THE CASTLE:

- Acknowledge the upside of your earning potential.

- When deciding to have a family, don't rule out keeping your job. At a minimum, maintain your professional network and complete any continuing education requirements to maintain any professional certifications you've earned (for example, registered architect, professional engineer, certified public accountant).

- The best way to secure your financial future is to stay in the workforce in some capacity, even when raising a family. You need to remain relevant and keep your skills up to date.

Part Two

A NEW SOVEREIGNTY: TAKING CONTROL OF YOUR FINANCIAL LIFE

Four
Budgeting and Banking Basics: Keeping Your Crown on Straight

In fairy tales, the path to endless bliss is fairly straightforward: First, slay the dragon. Second, inherit the land. But in real life, there are a few more steps involved. When it comes to your personal economy, it's hard to plan for the future when you don't know much about the present. So the first step is getting a handle on your current money situation.

This is what personal budgeting is all about. It isn't hocus-pocus. There is no get-rich-quick potion. Learning how to **budget,** however, can go a long way in creating financial magic in your future. When should you begin budgeting? Ideally, as soon as you get your first job, or even before that so you'll know the minimum salary that you can accept to meet your required living expenses.

You may or may not have learned about budgeting in school, but you did learn addition and subtraction. That's all you need to know for this chapter. The hard part isn't the math; it's the discipline to stick to the budget, which we will get to in a moment. Let's begin with some basics.

Money In versus Money Out

Budgets are also called **cash flow** statements, as in "you need to know where your cash is flowing to and from." On one side of the equation is the money that comes in, appropriately called "income." Presumably, this is earned income from your occupation, but it could also include monetary gifts (from your parents or other family members, for example); an inheritance; income from investments, an eBay business or rental property; or **alimony,** if you are divorced. Regardless of where it comes from, you need to know how much it is.

On the other side of the equation is the money that is going out and where it's going, sometimes referred to as "outflow." What are your expenses? I get it, keeping track of how much you're spending and what you spend it on may not be as much fun as a magic carpet ride but it's critical to taking control of your finances. To help you get started, see Additional Resources at the end of this book for useful websites that will help you manage your budget online, compare bank offerings, and provide lots of financial calculators to help you plan your savings over various time periods. You may want to invest in an accounting software program like Quicken or Microsoft Money, or create your own worksheet. I've included a sample of a general list of "Life's Expenses" in Appendix III. Not all of them will apply to you; however, this list will get you thinking about every expense you have.

Essential versus Discretionary Expenses

Now let's break down the general categories of expenses. Some expenses are **essential** to making your way in the world. You need a place to live. You need groceries and toiletries. You need a cell phone and probably a computer. You need a source of transportation other than a pumpkin carriage with a horse and driver. Depending on where you live, this might be as inexpensive as a bus pass. If public transportation isn't an option, you will need a car or access to a ride sharing service like Uber, Lyft or Zipcar. If you've got a car, you will need funds for car insurance, maintenance and gas.

Other expenses are **discretionary,** meaning that you have more control over whether you incur them. These expenses are not considered essential and include things like entertainment, gym memberships, kickass boots, cocktail dresses and having the jeweler buff and polish your crown. If it turns out that your income doesn't cover your outflow, then these expenses are where you have some options for cutting back. Keep in mind that even small expenditures can add up. Forego that venti mocha Frappuccino every weekend at Starbucks, for example, and you'll be on your way to saving about $100 a month.

Fixed versus Variable Expenses

Now let's look at categories for tracking these types of expenses. Some expenses are **fixed,** which means that they don't change from month to month. These are items like rent, a car payment, mobile phone plan, Internet service, and medical insurance (if your employer doesn't cover it and you have to pay outright). Other expenses are **variable;** they aren't the same amount every time you pay them. These include things like your grocery bill, the price of a tank of gas, your electric bill and repairs to your vehicle. Fixed costs are in your control and variable ones aren't; however, there is usually a range within which they will fluctuate, and this can be accounted for in your monthly budget. Payment schedules for these variable expenses can vary, too. Some are paid monthly, others quarterly and others annually.

A quick way of thinking about your expenses is this: Essential expenses are fixed or variable. Discretionary expenses are always variable; you can spend a lot, some or none.

The Benevolent Ruler: Charitable Giving

Depending on your worldview, charitable giving can be an essential or discretionary expense, fixed or variable. Some religious organizations strongly encourage their members to tithe 10% of their income to their place of worship. Many companies participate in the United Way campaign in which you can designate a specific charity to receive funds that are automatically deducted from your paycheck. Of course, you can make contributions directly to organizations that are important to you and those contributions are frequently **tax-deductible.** Whether they are or not should be clearly stated in their literature or on their websites.

When making your charitable giving decisions, consider making larger donations to fewer organizations instead of small donations to many. This can be difficult since there are so many worthwhile nonprofits, but narrow your organizations of choice to just a handful. The benefit of this is that your donations can make more of an impact, with an added bonus that you get on the organization's radar and that provides other benefits as well. You might then be invited to donor-only events where you meet other people like you who are committed to the organization and its mission. You might also be invited to join the organization's board. Seats on nonprofit boards are generally unpaid positions; however, they build your experience, allow you to network with other board members, and perhaps eventually garner a paid position on a corporate board.

Keep the Cash Flowing

Even queens must live within their means. If your income isn't enough to cover your outflow, something has to give. You must either earn more, spend less or both. Let's tackle cutting back on spending, as that's the fastest way to positively impact the situation.

Start with those discretionary expenses and see what you can trim. Maybe it's spending less on dining out with friends or buying less "fast fashion" that you'll be throwing away by next season. If shaving those expenses is not enough, examine your fixed and variable costs. Maybe you could live in a less expensive home or apartment, or save grocery dollars by eating less expensive cuts of steak and seafood.

This may not seem easy or fun, but it can be. Managing money can be exciting and rewarding, especially if you get creative. For example, go to the movies on $5 Tuesdays as a nice mid-week break. Plan a regular in-home Netflix night with friends; ask them to bring the popcorn, Raisinettes and other snacks. Instead of purchasing books on Amazon or downloading music from iTunes, get acquainted with your local library to borrow e-books or podcasts. Look for discounts like it's your job. A simple Internet search of what you want to buy followed by "coupon" or "discount code" can result in promotional codes for discounts and free shipping. Every good queen knows how to negotiate so she can pay less and earn more. It turns out that virtually everything except the price of gas is negotiable.[31]

Don't get caught up in "keeping up with the Kardashians." That is so yesterday. Today's world is all about sustainability, preserving and protecting the land for the heirs of the Earth. Reduce. Reuse. Recycle. It's more and more about cost sharing, collaborating on expenses, upcycling and eschewing excessive materialism. There are always going to be people who have more and better things than you do; however, often the people who have a lot of cool stuff *don't* have money in the bank, but *do* have a lot of debt. It's easy to assume that people who have expensive things make a lot of money. The truth is, you don't have any idea how much money they have or how they got it. (They might have inherited money from their own royal family.)

Covering Banking Basics

After setting up your budget, the next thing you'll want to do is start a banking relationship. You can't keep your cash under the mattress; it's far lumpier than the pea that kept that princess awake. Get thee to the nearest royal bank and open a:

Checking account: This is the main account through which your money will be going in and out regularly. If you are working outside the home, most likely your paychecks will be deposited directly to this account. This is also the account from which you'll pay your bills. You'll need checks, an ATM/debit card, and online access.

Because there will be a lot of activity in this account, it's important to make sure that both you and the bank think you have the same amount of money. You'll need to keep your own accounting of transactions. Sometimes banks make mistakes and sometimes you will, too. This check-and-balance of your checking account is affectionately referred to as "balancing your checkbook." You don't have to balance it in

[31] For more on the topic of negotiating, read *Women Don't Ask* and *Ask For It* by Linda Babcock and Sara Leschever; learn more by investigating Carnegie Mellon University's Leadership and Negotiation Academy for Women.

your head. You can do it with paper and pencil or you can use software programs like Quicken, Microsoft Money or Mint.

Many of your bills can be paid online and most companies prefer this. There are two approaches: 1) Have the company deduct your monthly bill automatically from your bank account. For example, for your monthly mobile phone bill, you can authorize ABC Communications to deduct the money from your XYZ Bank checking account; or 2) Go online to XYZ Bank's website and send the money electronically to ABC Communications. You'll still need checks, though, because not everyone is set up for electronic payments and not everyone accepts cash. For instance, you'll probably write a check to pay your taxes if they haven't been withheld from your paycheck. You'll need cash to tip the hairstylist who makes your crown fit perfectly.

An increasingly popular way of paying people is through a company called Venmo (venmo.com), which allows you to pay individuals without cash or writing a check. It's designed more for paying individuals than businesses. Examples are splitting a lunch bill or paying a friend for half of a cab or Uber fare. You transfer money from your bank account to your Venmo account then Venmo transfers the money from your account to your friend's Venmo account. I'm not endorsing Venmo, just giving it as an example; there are also other services like Apple Pay and PayPal.

Savings account: This will be your checking account's partner in helping you manage your money. It's the place to keep money that you don't need for your monthly expenses but want to have access to should you need it. In that way, it serves as your **Emergency** or **Personal Security Fund** (more about those soon). It's best to have a "stash of cash" for an emergency or anything unplanned for which you need cash on short notice, such as car and home repairs not covered under warranty or by insurance. It includes money that you might need to tide you over between jobs, in case you get laid off or decide to quit. Or perhaps you need a new place to live because of a month-to-month lease ending.

Your Emergency Fund should total between three and six months of your living expenses. Since you've done your budget, you now have a solid idea how much that is, but your personality comes into play here a bit, too. The more conservative your temperament, the more funds you'll want to keep in this account. If you're a worrier, you will want at least six months of expenses. On the other hand, if you're more confident in the speed with which you can replace the money needed to cover unexpected expenses, three months might do.

A savings account is a reminder to do just that: save. The sooner you get into the habit of feeding part of your income to the royal coffers on a consistent basis, the easier it becomes. It should be a way of life, something that is not optional. Why? Because it's critical to your long-term financial security. I've found that people have good intentions to start saving when they get their next raise or a new job. They think they'll be able to save whatever's left at the end of the month, but that never happens. The more money we make, the more (and more expensive) stuff we buy. An added benefit of having a savings account is that the bank pays you interest. In today's world of very low interest rates, the amount you earn is pretty small; however, it's more than you'll get in your checking account.

Online banking makes it easy to transfer money to different accounts. NOTE: You want to be transferring money FROM your CHECKING account TO your SAVINGS account. The name of the game is "saving." I can't stress that enough. It is a fundamental component of your budget. Suffice to say that the more you can automate your savings, the better off you're going to be. Most companies today direct deposit their employees' paychecks. You could have 80% put in your checking account and 20% put into savings. By doing so, you're challenging yourself to live on less than your full income. If you absolutely need to use the other 20%, you can get it from the savings account, but the goal is to try to spend less. Saving 20% of your income will set you on your way to eventually building a queen's ransom. When you get a raise or bonus, set some of that aside, too. You're already living on the pre-raise amount, so you know you can do it.

How and How Much?

Now that you've got your basic bank accounts set up to handle your most immediate cash needs, it's time to start planning for the short-, mid- and long-term. Again, start with your end goals so that you can match your money with your timeframe. This will enable you to know how much you'll need and when you'll need it. Here are some examples:

For the Short-Term

CAR Fund. If you need a car to get to work, you'll want something safe and reliable, but you don't need a luxury sedan. "Need" and "luxury" are not words that go together. Start comparison-shopping for a car that will meet your lifestyle. For example, if you have a long commute, you need especially good gas mileage or a long-lived battery for your electric car. Keep in mind that cars require maintenance and repairs. This is especially important because you're going to have your car a long time (think 10 years or 100,000 miles). The older it gets, the more repairs it needs. The more expensive the car, the more costly the parts and the more it costs to insure it. (We'll get into car loans and insurance in the chapters to come.)

EDUCATION Fund. If you think you'll need any kind of education to advance your career or keep your skills current so that you remain relevant, put some money away. Ideally, your company will invest in your continuing education and pay for courses related to your job. Either way, upgrading your skills may be a good idea and is always a good investment. Student loans are an option, but often their interest rates are high. (We'll talk more about that later, too.) Scholarships and grants are options, as well, but think of them as "icing on the cake."

VACATION Fund. It's true that money can buy you the best experiences (not just material things). Memories and photographs from a great vacation can be relived repeatedly, whereas the immediate gratification you get from buying a new gadget is fleeting. So where and when do you want to go? The world is a queen's playground. If you don't have money saved yet for a Royal Caribbean cruise (what else?) or a getaway to a land of castles like Ireland or Germany, then take a stay-cation. Stay home and sleep in. Be a tourist in your own town. Do all the things that you would do if you were entertaining a guest visiting from out of the area. Watch movies that you've always wanted to see, but haven't had time. Or go to a day spa and be treated like royalty. Maybe take a big trip every two or three years and in the off years, a financially savvy queen like you might want to learn more about all the corners of your own queendom.

For the Mid-Term

FIRST HOME Fund. For most people, buying a home is part of the American dream. If you want to buy a house, you'll need money for a **down payment,** and the amount of the down payment depends on how big of a house you want. Like a car though, houses have maintenance, repairs and insurance; plus, they require furniture and furnishings. The bigger the house, the more all of those things add up. They will need to be part of your planning and budget. (Along with auto and education loans, we'll cover the details of home **financing** later.)

For the Long-Term

RETIREMENT Fund. This is a challenge since many people don't begin thinking about their long-term goals until their mid-thirties. By then you've been working for a while. You're probably able to assess your career aspirations and the upward earning potential your position and industry will provide. You might have children and time begins to fly by. Suddenly, you can see 65 or 67 on the horizon. The good news is that when you're still in your thirties, you've got another 30 to 35 years to get where you want to go. And when it comes to saving, time is a critical factor. We'll get more into this in a later chapter, but for now just know that retirement funding needs to be part of your budget/savings plan. Most likely, you won't be doing this with a bank savings account; there are better options.

Once you start to accumulate funds from saving and taking care of personal financial business, your **net worth** will begin to grow, which is the subject of our next chapter.

ONCE UPON A TIME:
LUCY

Lucy is very goal oriented, but she isn't sure what she wants to be when she grows up. She's always been interested in human behavior so she decided to major in psychology. Her college career counselor advised that having a psychology major provides a foundation for many careers in addition to becoming a therapist. After all, knowing how the human mind works is useful no matter what field she might eventually choose.

Since health insurance was such a hot issue when she graduated, Lucy got a job at an insurance company. Just getting started in her career, Lucy first needs an Emergency Fund. To this point, her parents have been her source of cash in an emergency but she's an adult now. She needs to be prepared in case her job doesn't work out and she wants to (or is forced to) leave. Lucy also needs to replace her junker of a car, so a Car Fund is a necessity. She's been considering a Honda or Subaru for their modest cost, safety records and size. She figures she'll spend about $25,000 no matter what model she selects.

Next on Lucy's mind is a Vacation Fund. She's always wanted to travel and loved to get away to the beach when she was in school or with her family during the summer. She considers that to be a necessity and a beach vacation is definitely part of the plan. Maybe the Caribbean? The Bahamas? As soon as Lucy became eligible for her retirement plan at work, she signed up. She was surprised how little it affected her take-home pay. After a few years, having taken care of these essentials, she'll start to think about home ownership, but she's not quite ready for that. All in due time.

KEYS TO THE CASTLE:

- Get comfortable with budgeting and creating a simple cash flow statement.

- Determine how much it costs you to live by tracking expenses. This way, you'll know how much you can save or what adjustments you need to make to be sure your income exceeds your out-go. Remember that living within your means is essential to your long-term financial security.

- Set up your bank accounts: checking for your day-to-day cash management and savings for your Emergency Fund. Your savings account will also serve as the seeds to fund your mid-term goals (like Jack's beans for the beanstalk).

- Saving is a critical part of your budget. Don't leave it to chance. Start small, if needed, but start. Automate it if you can.

- Identify your goals: what you want, when you want them and how much they will cost.

- Start thinking about retirement now while time is on your side.

Five

Net Worth: How Much is the Coin of the Realm?

Any good queen is worth her weight in gold and will want to keep tabs on her financial value to reign effectively over her personal queendom. That means you.

Your **net worth,** as it's called, is basically a calculation of how much you're worth in monetary terms at a particular point in time. The details of one's net worth are typically spelled out on a **personal financial statement** or **balance sheet**. These documents illustrate your current financial position, including a summary of what you own and what you owe. (Free online templates are available to create a net worth statement. Simply Google "simple net worth statement template." Microsoft Excel has a very simple spreadsheet; I've included it below).

So why is it necessary to know your net worth? By calculating it over time, you'll be able to chart your progress in growing your personal wealth. This can lead to a positive snowball effect. The more improvement you see, the more motivated you will become to have it continue to grow. Seeing the big picture will help you to make thoughtful decisions about where to spend your money.

The left column lists what you own, or your **assets.** A **liquid** asset is cash or something that can be turned into cash quickly. When you're young and just starting out, the left side might only include your bank checking and savings accounts. Include your car and anything else you have that has a monetary value. It's okay to approximate. If you've contributed to a retirement plan at work, include that, too.

Queen

Estimated Net Worth

December 31

Estimated Net Worth: | **$50,000**

Liquid Assets		Liabilities	
Cash or Cash Equivalent		**Loan Balances**	**Estimated Value**
Checking Account	$10,000	Mortgage	$80,000
Savings Account	10,000	Student Loan	10,000
		Car Loan	10,000
Investments		**Other Debt**	
ABC Retirement Plan	10,000	Other Debt	N/A
Liquid Assets Total:	**$30,000**		
Non-Liquid Assets			
House	100,000		
Car	20,000		
Non-Liquid Assets Total:	**$120,000**		
Total Assets:	**$150,000**	**Liabilities Total:**	**$100,000**

The right column is where you list what you owe. These are also called your **liabilities.** They are the debts for which you are responsible and include things like student loans, a car loan, credit card debt, and anyone to whom you owe money. Of course, as ruler of the land, your goal is to own more than you owe . . . a lot more. Net worth can be a negative number if the opposite is true: when you owe more than you own. You absolutely don't want that.

Aside from having these statements handy for your personal

benefit, banks and lending institutions also use them when you're applying for **credit,** such as loans or a **mortgage.** It gives the loan officer the information necessary to easily understand your financial situation and determine if you qualify for a loan. (We'll get into this more in the next chapter.)

You'll want to update your net worth statement at least annually so that you can see your progress and (hopefully!) watch your net worth increase. Some people prepare them as of December 31st of the prior year; others do it as they are gathering their tax information. A net worth statement is also a great way to keep track of all your accounts in one easy place.

Truly, What Do You Own?

Did you know that there are different ways of owning things? For most people, there are mainly two: By yourself (individually) or with someone else (jointly).

Individually. These are assets that are solely in your name. You and you alone get to decide what happens to them. You are also the only person responsible for any debts attached to these assets; for example, your car and car loan.

Jointly With Rights of Survivorship. These assets are commonly referred to by the acronym **JTWROS.** What this means is that you and another person (or people) own the account. If something happens to you, the asset becomes the property of the remaining owners. Sometimes a parent and adult child have a joint checking account so that the child can help the parent manage their expenses while alive then receive the money directly upon the parent's passing. Married couples typically own their house jointly so that if something happens to either of them, the house automatically becomes the property of the survivor. Sometimes couples have a "yours, mine and ours" philosophy when handling their money, where each person has an account titled individually and one account that they share jointly.

Ideally, you and your co-owners jointly decide what to do with the assets. For bank accounts, any one of the owners can withdraw from the account without the permission of the other owners. The other bank account owners won't be notified that some or all the money has been withdrawn from the account. In technical terms, accounts like this are called "OR" accounts because one owner or another can act on the account independently of the other(s.)

For investment accounts, any one of the owners can make decisions on how to invest the money in the account, but none of the owners can withdraw the money without notifying the other owners. If any money is withdrawn from the account, it will be disbursed to all the owners together. These are considered "AND" accounts.

ONCE UPON A TIME: ALEXANDRA

Alexandra's career as a medical researcher afforded her a decent salary. Accordingly, she was able to pay cash for her car and make a sizeable down payment when buying her townhouse. She's single and ambivalent about getting married, so she relies on herself for her financial security.

After several years of working in research, Alexandra decided that she wanted to be a doctor. This was a huge decision, as it would affect her finances in a few different ways:

1. She would be taking on a lot of student loan debt.
2. She would not be working while in school so she would not be saving, either.
3. A fair amount of time would pass before she would be able to start saving again.

Nevertheless, Alexandra was up for the challenge and decided to embark on becoming a physician. Since heart disease is the number one killer of women, Alexandra specialized in cardiology. Her goal was to become a heart surgeon. Upon graduation, she was immediately hired by a large regional hospital.

The investment in her education was a good financial decision, as Alexandra now makes twice as much money as a surgeon than she did as a researcher. Having committed to aggressively getting her finances under control upon graduating, Alexandra paid off her student loans in half the time expected while putting as much as she could into her hospital's retirement plan. Within a few years of earning her MD, she had built her assets back to where they were before medical school, so her net worth was just as healthy as the patients she was serving.

KEYS TO THE CASTLE:

Know your net worth and update this statement regularly. This is the starting point from which you'll manage and grow your financial security.

Be clear on what you own individually and, therefore, control — and what you own jointly and how much control you have over those assets.

Six
Debt: Owning the Crown Free and Clear

When it comes to personal finances, long-term financial **sovereignty** comes from being out of debt. The less money you're paying someone else is more money that you have for yourself. Staying out of debt means, quite simply, not borrowing money. But there are instances where taking on debt might be unavoidable, such as when you decide to:

- buy things you need, like a car or a stove and refrigerator.
- improve your opportunities with education and career training.
- increase your net worth with something that's going to hold or increase in value, like a house.

Again, let's differentiate needs from wants. Doing so may be unpleasant but it isn't difficult.

Things You Need: You probably need, for instance, a car to get to work. You need appliances to wash and dry your clothes. These are considered **durable goods,** as they are expected to last for a while. If you don't have the cash on hand, taking loans for these items is a necessary evil. You will want to:

- buy the best value you can find; that is, the highest quality for a reasonable cost.
- know the true cost and value of the item.
- understand the interest rate you'll be charged for the loan, the monthly payment and the length of time you'll be paying. (You'll want these to be as low or as small as possible.)

Things You Want: Don't go into debt to take a European vacation or buy a boat. I know, you're hoping I'd tell you that since you work hard, you should indulge yourself because you deserve it. Well, you do deserve it; you just need to save for it. I'm not talking about self-deprivation. You can't spend your whole life delaying gratification until you retire. Life's too short, even for a queen. There are lots of ways, however, to have fun that don't require breaking the bank. Keep your eye on the ultimate prize: long-term financial security. The long-term is comprised of a lot of short terms. You may want that $100,000 Porsche convertible today but keep in mind that it shaves off the amount of money you'll have in the long run.

Credit: History, Rating and Report

Although it would be ideal to save in advance for any purchases you need to make so that you can pay for them in full, that's not always practical. You'll probably need a car before you have the cash to pay for it, for instance. You also might want to stop paying rent and buy a house. Big purchases like these often require that you "buy on credit" – or, borrow money from a bank or financing institution.

Let's talk "plastic" for a minute. The good thing about credit cards is that they are usually easy to get, which can be helpful for young adults just starting out. Credit card companies will offer to open accounts for you before almost anyone else because they have a strong hunch that your parents will bail you out if you run up your credit card balance. Additionally, you have a long credit life ahead of you; that means lots of years of interest payments for the credit card companies. As you use your card and pay off the balance each month, you are demonstrating that you are a responsible borrower. You are building a **credit history.** To do that, you need to have loans in your own name without a parent or anyone else co-signing. You can't just be named on someone else's account. If you pay your bill on time, the credit card company will increase your spending limit. Having a higher limit doesn't mean you need to spend more; it is just helpful to know that you can borrow a larger amount in case of emergencies.

A credit history is how you establish a **credit rating,** which is a way for financial institutions to determine how much money they are willing to lend you and at what price (i.e., interest rate). The better your credit rating, the lower the interest rate a bank or financing company will charge you. A credit rating is also called a **credit score.** The best score is 850, but somewhere in the 700s is quite good. How can you determine your credit score? There are three companies that issue **credit reports**: Experian, Equifax and TransUnion. According to the government, you are entitled to one free report annually that details your credit rating from all three companies. (Visit annualcreditreport.com.) This is important since you'll want to be sure the records are accurate, as well as making sure no one is using your identity to take out loans in your name for their own nefarious purposes. (It happens these days.)

Interest Rates

Interest is, in a phrase, the cost of money. Just like anything else you buy, when you're shopping for a loan, you want the cost to be as low as possible and the price to be competitive. So, just like anything else, you're wise to comparison shop. Think of when you're buying a car. You want the most value for your money. You want quality at a competitive price that meets your needs. To match that, you want a loan at a competitive price that meets your needs.

Federal law requires lenders to disclose the interest rates they charge; you will often see these displayed in big, bold print. Interest rates fluctuate. In the United States, the lowest rate that financial institutions charge their very best customers is called the **Prime Rate.** Over the past 35 years, the Prime Rate has been as low as 3.25% and as high as 13%. Frequently, interest rates are quoted relative to the Prime Rate. For example, your rate might be "Prime plus one percent."

Of course, when shopping for a loan, you will want to know the interest rate that you'll be charged and if it's going to change over the course of the loan. If it's never going to change, it's a **fixed rate.** If it can change, it's called a **variable** or **adjustable rate.** If it's the latter, you will want to know what would cause your rate to change and how much it might fluctuate. You'll want to have a good sense of whether you can afford the maximum rate and, accordingly, the maximum payment.

So, what happens once you obtain the loan? Well, the goal is to pay it off as soon as possible. If you have more than one loan, it's preferable to pay off the ones with the highest interest rates first. Generally, the continuum of interest rates from highest to lowest is:
1. Credit cards
2. Car loans
3. Education loans
4. Mortgages

This is not set in stone. Interest rates on education loans can vary tremendously based on which year of your education they were used. Depending on your income, the interest on education loans can be tax-deductible. Still, the strategy remains the same: Pay off the highest interest rates first.

When you are out shopping for a vehicle and other material items like mattresses and appliances, keep an eye out for zero percent financing opportunities. Car dealers frequently offer deals like this but other vendors do, too, even for professional services, like dental and eye care. If you haven't been able to save enough to buy something in full, zero percent financing is the next best thing. Zero percent allows you to borrow money without the cost of interest. You're paying the same price you would if you paid cash, but you can spread your payments out over time.

Sometimes, credit card companies will offer low interest rates if you consolidate all of your credit card balances onto their card. This might be a good idea but read the fine print carefully. The low rate might be for just a limited time, like the first six months; then it may increase dramatically such that the rate is higher than what you were paying before consolidating! The last thing you want is more money being charged at a higher interest rate. If you don't understand the terms, ask to speak with the financing manager to clarify. Unfortunately, the inequity between men and women when it comes to the cost of things applies to lending, too: women, on average, pay more for mortgages than men — even more reason to shop for a competitive rate.[32]

....

©Glasbergen
GLASBERGEN

"And they lived happily ever after until the credit card bills arrived and they realized they couldn't afford to be quite so happy."

A Word About Tax Deductibility

A detailed discussion of taxes is outside the scope of this book, but in general, things described as **tax-deductible** work in your financial favor. Essentially, tax deductibility means that you can reduce your taxable income in some way, which means paying less in income taxes. Generally speaking:

....

[32] Cheng, Ping and Lin, et. al., "Do Women Pay More for Mortgages?" *Journal of Real Estate, Finance and Economics* (October 11, 2011).

- Interest paid on home mortgages is tax-deductible.
- Interest paid on student loans is tax-deductible in some instances.
- Interest paid on car loans and credit card debt is never tax-deductible.

The first and second items might be referred to as "good" debt and the third one as "bad" debt. So, what does that mean? One is naughty and the other nice? Not really but tax-deductible debt is better than not tax-deductible and the interest rates tend to be lower.

For Better . . .

Some types of debt are better than others and the best type – as we've noted above – is tax-deductible. Since you're probably only going to be borrowing money for things like a chateau or an education, the IRS is willing to give you an extra benefit for that. Any interest that is tax-deductible is preferable to debt that isn't because the true **after-tax** cost to you is less than it would be if it weren't deductible. The formula is: Interest rate x (1 - your tax rate.)

By way of example, let's say you want to buy a house and your **mortgage** rate is 5%. Because the interest is tax-deductible, your true after-tax cost is less than 5%; how much less depends on your tax bracket. Let's say you're in the 24% tax bracket. Here's the math: 5% x (1 - 24%) = 5% x 76% = 3.8%. Obviously, 3.8% is less than 5%, so the tax-deductible loan costs less.

You won't really "see" the benefit of the tax deduction until you prepare your income tax return, but it's there. Keep in mind, though, that even if the rates are low and the interest is tax-deductible, it's still money you're paying someone. As mentioned above, interest on home mortgages is tax-deductible. In general, houses have been a way to help people save, a useful way to force them to build an asset. NOTE: Some people use the equity in their homes as their Emergency Fund. If you own a house, you can borrow against the equity in it. **Equity** is the difference between what your home is worth and what you owe on it.

. . . Or Worse

Credit Cards: Although you need a credit card to make your way through modern life, credit card debt is the worst kind of debt. Not only is the interest not tax-deductible, the rates are the highest when compared to virtually any other type of loan you can get. Even when the Prime Rate is only 3.25%, interest rates on credit cards can be 20%. To give you an idea of how this impacts you, let's do the math.

Suppose you take out two loans, both for $20,000 for five years. ABC Bank is going to charge you 5%; XYZ Credit Card Company is charging you 20%. Over 5 years, you will pay $2,645 in interest to ABC Bank and $11,793 in interest to XYZ Credit Card Company. How crazy is that? You're paying more than $11,793 in interest to get $20,000!

It's really difficult to get out of credit card debt with interest rates that high, even for a monarch. Not only does the interest continue to accumulate, you will have to continue to buy stuff (groceries, clothes, etc.) while paying for the stuff you've already bought. On top of that, it's enticing to only make the minimum payment since it's prominently displayed at the top of the account statement. Remember, the goal is to pay off your credit card in full every month. Paying anything less than the full balance due makes it very challenging to get out from under the burden that credit card debt creates. There's no question that you need a credit card. When used responsibly, they are just one of the arrows in your financial quiver (the operative phrase being "used responsibly").

Car Loans: Although you'll probably need a loan for your first carriage when you're starting out, don't buy into the idea that you'll always need one. People do pay cash for their cars and you want to be one of them. This is not the "American way" of acquiring a motor vehicle that you see in car advertising; nevertheless, it is possible. Here's one way to do it: Standard car loans are for five years, but plan to keep your car for 10 years. In year six, after you've paid the loan, redirect your payments to your savings account. For the next five years, you'll be saving to pay cash for your next car. Maybe you won't be able to save enough for all of it, but when combined with the trade-in value of your old car, you won't need as a big of a car loan as you would if you hadn't been saving all along.

ONCE UPON A TIME: ISABELLE AND AINSLY

Isabelle and Ainsly invested in themselves by furthering their education. Unfortunately, this meant that they had to take on some student loans. They also needed a place to live and some furnishings for their apartment, so they sprung for some things on their credit cards. It was nice to have a comfy bed, fine linens, a big-screen TV and a beautiful dining table, but these purchases got Isabelle and Ainsly into financial hot water. This was not solely their fault, as they were enticed by the credit card offers they received while they were still in school that made them feel "grown up." Friends and family members further advised them that they needed to build a credit history and credit cards are the way to start. They thought that buying these material items was a smart thing to do.

What these well-meaning friends didn't tell them (or what they were told but didn't listen to) is that they should pay their monthly balances in full every month. With interest rates of 12% on their student loans and 18% on their credit cards, they found that most of their monthly income was going to paying their loan balances.

Isabelle and Ainsly are smart though. To get out from under this burden, they put themselves on a strict budget and looked for opportunities to consolidate their debts at lower interest rates to reduce their payments. With a plan and a strategy, they were able to pay off their loans much faster than they originally thought, thereby being able to kick back and truly relax on that new leather sofa and enjoy binge-watching Netflix with friends on their HD TV.

KEYS TO THE CASTLE:

- Make thoughtful choices about how you spend your money; don't purchase things you don't need before you have the money to pay for them.

- Shop around for the lowest interest rate possible for the amount of money you need to borrow.

- Pay your debts on time to keep a good credit rating. The better your credit rating, the lower the interest rates you'll be charged. Check your credit rating annually to make sure it's accurate.

- Pay your credit card balances in full every month.

- Evaluate the true cost of any loan: the percentage interest rate, whether it's tax-deductible or not, and the total dollar value of the interest you'll pay over the term of the loan.

Seven

Insurances: Protecting Your Castle and Other Assets

You're building your life as a young royal and thoughtfully acquiring the things that you need, all the while keeping an eye on your future prosperity. Now that you own some things and are becoming adept at keeping financial track of it all, the next step is knowing how best to protect it.

Unless you've got all the king's horses and all the king's men, you probably need to have some forms of insurance to protect your queenly assets. Insurance is a way to guard against possible expenses that would be catastrophic to your financial situation. It is the basis of a sound financial plan.

Simply stated, you MUST protect what you already have as you continue to build your financial empire. There are lots of different types of insurances (which we will cover here) to protect against the various financial risks you may face. There are also many different factors to consider in addressing your unique needs. The best thing to do is to work with qualified insurance agents who can help you craft a "risk management plan" for your situation. You can do it yourself online, but I don't recommend it. This is an area where what you don't know can hurt you. When buying insurance, it's important that the policy covers the risks you face. The last thing you want is to file a **claim** only to find that it's not covered.

The Modern Day Moat

Most people don't like thinking about insurance because it implies that something bad might happen. Unfortunately – or, fortunately – you only "get your money back" if something goes wrong, but there's no reason to be overly pessimistic. Only insure against things that can be disastrous to your financial situation, like exorbitant healthcare costs, damage to your home or car, and the possible inability to work or care for yourself in your golden years. Yes, it's unpleasant and certainly not glamorous, but dealing with difficult things is part of "adulting."

It's true, no one wants to pay for something they hope to never use. Understanding the importance of insurance just requires a little attitude adjustment. It's simply the price you pay to offload the risk you face — either from poor health, death or the destruction of your personal property. Think about it this way: if you never have to use it, you've gotten the best value out of it. In other words, you never want your house to burn down such that you need to make a claim on your homeowner's policy. You never want to get in a car accident such that you need to file a claim on your auto insurance. You never want to get so sick that you have to worry about what the maximum limit is on your health insurance. In the most extreme case, you don't want to die to have someone collect the death benefit on your life insurance. Sometimes, however, bad things happen that aren't your fault. Again, you only want to buy insurance for circumstances that would be disastrous to your financial situation.

The less likely you are to file a claim, the lower your cost for buying insurance (in other words, your **premium** payment). The chances of a young healthy person dying are pretty small, so the premiums for life insurance are low; however, it does happen and it can devastate the financial situation of anyone who is dependent on you. The greater the probability that you'll use the insurance, the more money the insurance company is going to charge you. This makes sense since the insurance carrier needs to collect more money now if the chances are higher that they are going to be paying out money later. They need to be compensated to cover the risk they face of paying a claim.

Sometimes, when an insurance company pays a claim to a policyholder, others will remark that the insured "was lucky because her insurance covered it." That woman wasn't lucky. She performed prudent risk management. She paid premiums to cover this potential situation. There was no luck involved; just mature, financially sound decision making to share the risk of **loss** with a financial institution that can afford to pay the claim.

Your Human Capital

The first thing you need to insure is yourself, especially to provide for anyone who might be relying on you financially. You probably didn't list yourself as an asset on the left side of your net worth statement. That's understandable and it would be kind of weird if you did. It's hard to "quantify" or put a value on yourself. Nevertheless, the value is there; it's your human capital. Think of it this way: If you had a machine in your closet that printed money, you would definitely insure it against loss. Well, YOU are the money machine because you have earning power!

Health Insurance

When we're young, we feel invincible and immortal. Still, most people know that they need health insurance, no matter how old or how much money they have. If you are struck by a serious, chronic illness, the cost of your care can be enormous. Health insurance protects you financially, since it covers expenses that have the potential to be catastrophic. Prescription drugs for chronic but not life-threatening conditions can cost a fortune. Medical costs add up quickly and can dramatically weigh down the right side of the ledger. It's going to be one of the biggest line items in your budget. If your company offers a health insurance plan – called "group" insurance – chances are that's going to be the least expensive of your options.

Essentially, there are three phases to medical insurance benefits:

1. **Co-pay.** These are expenses for which both you and the insurance company share in the cost. For example, you might have to pay $15 when you go to the doctor and the insurance carrier pays the rest of the doctor's charges. Typically, co-pays are lower for primary care visits and higher for visits to a specialist.

2. **Co-insurance.** If you need more care after your initial visit, you and the insurance carrier share costs on a percentage basis up to a stated maximum. It is common for you to be responsible for 20% of the costs and the insurance carrier to pay 80% up to a maximum of $5,000.

3. **Full benefits.** Once you reach the maximum out-of-pocket, the insurance company pays 100% of the rest of your expenses up to a maximum of, say, $1 million. After that, you're back to paying on your own.

Here's an example of how each of the above work together: You visit your primary care physician for a skin rash and pay $15. She sends you to a specialist, where you pay $25 for your initial visit. A course of treatment is prescribed that costs a total of $6,000. You and the insurance company split the cost up to $5,000; your share is $1,000 (which = 20% of $5,000.) After that, the insurance carrier pays for all your expenses up to a maximum of $1 million.

What's covered and not covered by health insurance policies varies and is complicated. Not all care is subject to **deductibles** and co-pays. Often preventative care, like physicals and mammograms, is covered at 100% by the insurance carrier – meaning that you don't have to pay anything. Visits to specialists often have co-pays.

HDHPs and HSAs: The future of medical insurance is unclear; however, we can only plan based on what we know today. Until changes are mandated on the national level, **high-deductible health plans (HDHPs)** paired with **health savings accounts (HSAs)** is one way the insurance carriers are trying to get a handle on their costs. These plans are just as they sound. Your deductible is high, maybe as high as $3,000 for yourself and $5,000 for your family; however, there are no co-pays. Once you've exhausted your deductible, the insurance company will start paying all of your costs.

In conjunction with HDHP, you'll have an HSA. Money will be deducted from your paycheck that will fund this HSA, and the money in this account will be used to satisfy your deductible. The advantage of paying your medical costs from an HSA is the tax benefit; the money that goes into the HSA is tax-deductible. To explain further: assume you are in the 24% income tax bracket and your doctor charges you $100 for an office visit. Here's what happens if you have an HSA and what happens if you don't.

- **If you do:** You have $100 deducted from your paycheck and deposited into your HSA to fund your out-of-pocket medical costs. You have a debit card for this account and use it to pay the doctor when you leave her office. You have $100 available that you never have to pay income tax on.
- **If you don't:** You don't have $100 deducted from your paycheck. You owe 24% tax on that money so that you only net $76; that's the amount deposited to your regular bank checking account. The doctor still charges you $100. You use the $76 after-tax money AND you must use another $24 from your bank account to pay the doctor's bill. (NOTE: That $24 is also after-tax money, so instead of $100 going into your HSA to pay the doctor's bill, you will have to earn $132 to pay the same bill with after-tax money.)

So, here's what each of these scenarios looks like:
- Using an HSA: $100 withheld from your paycheck →→→ $100 to pay the doctor
- With no HSA: $132 paid to you directly →→→ $32 in income taxes →→→ $100 paid to the doctor

Disability Insurance
The purpose of disability insurance is to provide an income to you if you can't work. It is only for people who are generating income from paid

employment – either employed by someone else or running their own business. Disability insurance is not inexpensive but that's because you're more likely to become disabled than to die or have your house burn down. It's likely that you'll make a claim on the policy and the insurance carrier is on the hook. Since their risk is higher, your premium is higher.

But, there's good news. Many companies offer at least a minimal amount of group disability insurance for their employees. In general, the rates are lower than if you bought the coverage on your own (just like health insurance). The benefits aren't as good as individual policies, but they do offload some of your risk and at a more affordable price.

Standard group short-term disability benefits provide 60% of your salary for up to 26 weeks. Many times, these are partnered with long-term disability policies that start after 26 weeks and pay 60% of your salary for two years. Here's where the devil is in the details: Group long-term disability insurance policies often have **any occupation disability** coverage. This means that the policy will pay provided you can't perform any job at all. On the other hand, individual disability policies often have **own occupation disability** coverage. This means that if you can't perform the specific job you currently have (or one requiring comparable skills and experience), you'll receive a benefit from the insurance company.

Life Insurance

If anyone is financially dependent on you, you need life insurance. Bad stuff happens to good people. Usually, it's unexpected. The time to buy insurance is when you aren't sick. When it comes to life, health, disability and long-term care insurance, it's not just money that buys it. It's both money and health. Once you're diagnosed with something, you no longer have the option of buying insurance to manage the risk. And the younger and healthier you are, the less expensive it's going to be. The goal is to be proactive. Think of it as taking advantage of the opportunity that good health provides.

There are five main components to every life insurance policy:

1. **Insured.** The person upon whose death the insurance company will pay the death benefit.
2. **Owner.** The person who controls the policy. Usually the owner is the same as the insured, but not always.
3. **Death benefit.** The amount of money that will be paid to the beneficiary upon the insured's death.
4. **Beneficiary.** The person who will receive the death benefit upon the insured's passing.
5. **Premium.** The amount of money paid to the insurance company now for the death benefit to be paid later.

Essentially, there are two different types of life insurance: term and permanent.

Term Insurance: This is a type of life insurance you buy for a specified number of years – or, the term. Once the term ends, so does the insurance. If you have children and want to be sure money is available for their education, you might buy 25-year term insurance when they are born. This coordinates with the timeframe for when most students complete their higher education. In the event of your untimely demise within those 25 years, the life insurance death benefit could be used to pay these higher education costs. Once they have completed their education, you no longer need the insurance for that purpose.

Because you are young when you buy the coverage and the insurance carrier only pays a benefit if you die within 25 years, this type of coverage is less expensive than permanent insurance. If your health is good, insurance is cheap. A 35-year-old woman in relatively good health can buy 25 years of $250,000 term life insurance coverage for as little as $20/month and $500,000 of coverage for $35/month.

Permanent Insurance: Just as its name implies, **permanent insurance** policies are meant for you to keep your entire life. Since the insurance company will be paying a death benefit at some point, this type of coverage is more expensive than term insurance. There are three types of permanent insurance: whole life, universal life (or, flexible life) and variable universal life. What product is best for you depends on your needs and goals. **Universal life** policies provide the most options over the life of the policy; that's why they are also known as **flexible** or **adjustable life** insurance policies. Within a stated range, you can pay different amounts of premiums – more or less, depending on your cash flow at the time. They also allow you to take a loan against the policy. There are lots of moving parts to permanent insurance policies and working with an experienced insurance agent provides a lot of value when buying coverage.

Most permanent life insurance policies have a savings component to them. As you pay your insurance premiums, some of the money goes to pay the cost of insurance and some goes into a savings portion of the policy; this is called the **cash value.** It can be a very effective way to help you save money since the cash value gets funded as part of your regular premium payment. Usually, you can borrow against the cash value at a modest interest rate for any reason if you want the money. This is unlike other loans where you might need to provide **collateral** for the loan, like a house or car.

Policies vary from company to company. If you work with a life insurance agent to purchase the coverage, they will help you determine what type is right for you. If you don't work with an agent, be sure to read the terms of the policy carefully to be sure you understand the details.

There's good news here, too, if you are an employee. Many companies provide some amount of life insurance for their employees. Sometimes, it's a flat amount; that is, everyone gets $100,000. Typically, it's some multiple of your earnings, like three times your salary. Get the details from your HR manager. This is a great starting point but you might need more than three times your salary. Remember, though, this insurance is contingent upon you staying with the same employer. That's an important thing to consider when developing your risk management plan.

If you're a stay-at-home spouse, don't underestimate the economic value you provide to your family. Think of all the work you do on a daily basis, particularly if you are a parent. There is a seemingly endless array of things that children need beyond food, clothing and housing. They need day care, doctors' appointments, haircuts, and help with homework; the list goes on and on. If your spouse travels, how much would it cost to have full-time childcare to cover overnight responsibilities if you could not fulfill them? Insurance can't replace you but it can help pay for the vital household services that are critical to keeping a family functioning.

Long-Term Care Insurance

Essentially, this is insurance to help pay for the care you'll need as you age. We'll get into more detail about this when we talk about retirement planning. (That's usually when this moves to the top of the list of insurances you'll need.)

....

©Glasbergen

**"Be home before midnight, Cinderella.
Your carriage insurance doesn't
cover pumpkins or mice!"**

The Royal Wares: Property and Casualty

Property and casualty insurance is what you need to protect your stuff and any harm you or your stuff causes other people. **Auto insurance** is a perfect example of this type of coverage. The car is the property you are protecting. If you get into an accident, you'll want to have it repaired or replaced. The casualty part of the insurance is the compensation that will be paid if you or someone else is hurt in the accident. Most state laws require a minimum amount of coverage for all vehicle owners. If the law didn't require it, most people wouldn't get car insurance. People just don't like to think that they'll get into an accident or damage their car. Simply put, with property and casualty insurance, after you satisfy the deductible, the insurance company covers the rest. The higher your deductible, the greater your share of the expenses. Since you'll be paying more if there's a claim against the policy, you'll pay less in premiums.

Renter's insurance: Before you own a home, your stuff (like your electronics, clothing and furniture) is probably your most valuable asset. If you don't own a home yet, consider **renter's insurance.** It's typically inexpensive – again, because the value of your stuff probably isn't that large. However, unless you want to buy (and have the money to buy) all new material goods, spend a few dollars insuring what you've got to protect it from theft and damage. Renter's insurance is very inexpensive compared to other types of coverage, and your premium might be as low as $100/year, depending on the value of your items.

Homeowner's insurance: Once you own a house, **homeowner's insurance** is a must. For most people, their home is their biggest asset. Accordingly, you need to protect yourself by insuring it against catastrophic risks. If you're going to borrow money from a bank or mortgage company to buy the house, they are going to require that you insure it. Once you build your net worth, you'll probably want to consider an **umbrella insurance** policy. Like its name suggests, an umbrella policy is additional insurance to cover any kind of claim caused by you or your property. An example of this is if someone slips on ice on the sidewalk in front of your house. They might sue you to pay for any medical care they need as a result.

Home ownership is another reason for life insurance. Some mortgages have life insurance attached to them so that if the borrower passes away before the loan is paid, then the mortgage will be satisfied. This is good for anyone who shares the house with you as they now have a debt-free place to live. You wouldn't want a friend, partner or child forced out of their home upon your passing. They'd be grieving your loss; you don't want to compound that by uprooting them. If the insurance pays off the mortgage, it would also free up their monthly cash flow by no longer having one of the largest monthly expenses most people have.

Cash Stash or Borrow: Your Own Personal Insurance
There are other ways to prepare for unexpected expenses outside of buying insurance. You could save a huge amount of cash so that you can pay for any emergency or tragedy that comes along (just don't store it under your queen-size mattress). That's called "self-insurance" or "self-funding." For most people, this is just not practical. You need your Emergency Fund to cover small, unexpected expenses (like a car repair or new furnace). But get used to the idea that you're always going to need insurance to cover the big things. It is a small price to pay relative to the size of the asset you're protecting, whether that's your car, your house or yourself. There are some risks, though, for which you can't buy a traditional insurance policy:

- **Divorce.** As I mentioned earlier, divorce is much more harmful to a woman's financial security than a man's. Depending on the state in which she lives and the skills and success of her legal counsel, a divorced woman might get significant assets and alimony to cover her living costs, or she might not.
- **Job loss.** In the world of downsizing, rightsizing and technological advances, people sometimes lose their jobs through no fault of their own. It might be a temporary situation or it might be long-term. In either case, the loss will have a financial impact of some kind on the family – anything from meeting daily living expenses to lost life or health insurance coverage to reduced savings.
The best protection for either of these risks is keeping your skills sharp and maintaining network relationships.

ONCE UPON A TIME: SOPHIE AND CARSON

Sophie and Carson met in graduate school. They both secured good jobs in the engineering field, got married and wanted to start a family. Once the kids came along, Sophie quit work and Carson's career continued to progress.

Carson's a great engineer but not so savvy when it comes to matters of insurance and finance. He doesn't believe in life insurance. He feels that if something happens to him, Sophie can go back to work. Similarly, he feels that since Sophie is a stay-at-home spouse and no longer brings earned income to the household, life insurance isn't necessary for her. Let's walk through a few scenarios:

First let's assume that Carson meets his untimely demise. The family is grieving; Sophie has lost her husband and the children have lost their father. Do the children need more care or less in this situation? Does anyone want Sophie to be forced to return to work to feed the family? How employable is Sophie at this point? Yes, she is an engineer by training and education, but are her skills current? Has she maintained her network so that she can get in front of the right people who can offer her a job? Chances are she can't earn a salary comparable to what Carson made. How will she pay for daycare? Who will do all the things she has been doing while *not* working outside the home?

On the other hand, let's assume Sophie meets her untimely demise and Carson is the widower. The children have just lost their mother and he has lost his wife. Can he continue to maintain his work schedule so that his career continues to thrive? What's he going to do for childcare during the day, especially if they don't have family in the area? What if travel is a big part of his job? Where does he find overnight childcare? How much does that cost?

Together, Sophie and Carson need to figure out what they want to have happen in each of these scenarios and attach dollar amounts to them. Would they want money to be available for the kids' education costs? Would they like to pay off any balance on the mortgage? Would they want to provide a way for the surviving spouse to have supplemental income since, in either situation, their daycare expenses are going to rise? Once they can identify their goals, they'll be able to determine the amount of life insurance they need. Then they can buy policies to meet their goals and budget.

KEYS TO THE CASTLE:

- Protect what you have. First, your health; second, your stuff.

- Insure against risks that will be catastrophic to your financial situation: life, health, disability, property and casualty (home and auto).

- Know the details of your policies: what's covered, for how long and for how much.

- Know what's not covered and what your maximum out-of-pocket will be to pay those things.

Eight

Saving: Filling the Imperial Coffers with Appropriate Investments for Your Goals

Wouldn't it be great if you could wave your scepter and all the money you need would spontaneously appear? Well, creating your golden nest egg takes a little more work than that, although it does involve a certain sort of "magic." In this chapter, we'll review the different types of investments you can use to work towards your various savings goals. First let's start with some basic concepts that you should know when building your financial dynasty.

Real Life Magic: The Rule of 72

As I mentioned earlier, the math involved in most investments is no more complicated than eighth-grade addition, subtraction, multiplication, division and percentages. With respect to percentages, being aware of the Rule of 72 is very helpful. Essentially, you can divide any number into 72 and you'll learn how long it will take to double your money. For example, if you're getting 3% on your investment, it will take 24 years for your money to double (72 ÷ 3 = 24). If you earn 7%, it will take 10.2 years (72 ÷ 7 = 10.2). If you earn 10%, it will take 7.2 years (72 ÷ 10 = 7.2).

. . and so on. The Rule of 72 is a very simple tool to help you make very rough estimates of how your money might grow.

This "rule" is just for illustrative purposes. It shows you that the higher the return, the shorter the time span for your money to increase in value. This will help you select appropriate investments to match your goals and the timeframes for meeting them.

Rate of Return	Years until you double your money	Rate of Return	Years until you double your money
2.00%	36.0	7.00%	10.2
3.00%	24.0	8.00%	9.0
4.00%	18.0	9.00%	8.0
5.00%	14.4	10.00%	7.2
6.00%	12.0		

Keep in mind, though, that there aren't many investments that guarantee high rates of return (like 7% or more) year in and year out. There is a love-hate relationship between risk and reward. The more risk you are willing to take, the more opportunity you have for a higher reward (that is, a higher **rate of return).** Yet it can also go the other way: the more risk you take, the more "opportunity" for your investment to go down in value.

Generally, the stronger the guarantee, the lower the rate of return. For example, bank savings accounts and CDs generally have the lowest rates of returns, but they are guaranteed to not lose money, as they are insured by the FDIC. On the other hand, returns in the stock market might average 8% to 10% over long periods, but there are no guarantees and sometimes the fluctuations from year to year are dramatic.

The Miracle of Compounding

The magic doesn't stop with the Rule of 72. There is also a noble principle of saving and investing called **compound interest.** Albert Einstein called it "the greatest mathematical discovery of all time." Essentially, it's when you earn interest on your interest. Let's say that you invest $10,000 at 3%. After a year, you've earned $10,300 [= 10,000 x 1.03]. In the next year, you earn 3% on the bigger amount of $10,300 for a total of $10,609 [= 10,300 x 1.03] and all you did was leave your money alone. Over time, it really adds up.

 ONCE UPON A TIME:
ELIZABETH

A very wealthy woman named Elizabeth hired a young man to work every day for a month mowing the lawns of her vast estate. She offered him two payment options: "I will pay you $1,000 per day for the next 31 days; or if you prefer, I will pay you one cent for the first day and for every day after that, double the amount you received the previous day."

The young man jumped at the offer of $1,000 per day because he immediately figured that his paycheck would be a sizeable $31,000. What this unlucky man failed to realize is that if he had opted for the generous daily compounding from that single penny, he would have extracted a 31-day salary of over $10 MILLION.[33]

If you think this seems farfetched, here's the math*:

....
[33] Ballard, Ednalou, CFP©, *Profit and Prosper: Tax, Estate and Investment Planning Strategies* (1988) 55-56.

Day 1	$0.01	Day 11	$10.24	Day 21	$10,485.76
Day 2	0.02	Day 12	20.48	Day 22	20,971.52
Day 3	0.04	Day 13	40.96	Day 23	41,943.04
Day 4	0.08	Day 14	81.92	Day 24	83,886.08
Day 5	0.16	Day 15	163.84	Day 25	167,772.16
Day 6	0.32	Day 16	327.68	Day 26	335,544.32
Day 7	0.64	Day 17	655.36	Day 27	671,088.64
Day 8	1.28	Day 18	1,310.72	Day 28	1,342,177.28
Day 9	2.56	Day 19	2,621.44	Day 29	2,684,354.56
Day 10	5.12	Day 20	5,242.88	Day 30	5,368,709.12
				Day 31	$10,737,418.24

Yes, it's an extreme example with 100% daily compounding and, yes, it dramatically illustrates the powerful tool of accruing interest on the interest you've already earned.

The performance information provided is not indicative of any particular investment. This is a purely hypothetical example of mathematical compounding at 100% and does not represent the past or future performance of any specific product or class of investments.

How Much Risk Can You Handle?

Once you've established your goals, the next thing you need to determine is how much risk you can handle with your hard-earned dollars. Just as your goals are unique, investing is also different for every individual. The investment plan that's right for you depends largely on the level of comfort that you have when it comes to risk. You can't completely avoid risk but it's possible for you to manage it. There are different kinds of risks.

Market Risk: In the investment world, market risk means how much fluctuation in value you can stand before panicking. How much risk you can take with your investments depends on your tolerance for volatility, as well as your timeframe. Typically, investors are grouped into three broad categories for the purposes of discussing risk tolerance:

- Aggressive: those who have a high degree of risk tolerance
- Moderate: those willing to accept a modest amount of risk
- Conservative: those who have low risk tolerance

These can be expanded to include "moderately aggressive" and "moderately conservative." (To determine what kind of risk taker you are, check out Appendix II.)

Investments fluctuate in value more when there is the potential for a greater return. Your investment might increase in value a lot or it may not and, in many situations, the possibility of losing your entire investment is a very real concern. Yes, you have the potential for higher returns; however, it doesn't matter how high the returns are if you can't sleep at night because you're worried about a decline in your **portfolio** (and, therefore, your net worth). In that situation, the higher potential return is probably too great a price to pay to offset the amount of sleep lost.

Generally, for longer-term goals (like when retirement is several years away) you have enough time to withstand market fluctuations. Time is on your side when it comes to saving and investing, both for compounding your investments and riding out the volatility; however, if market fluctuations make you crazy, then you must adjust your investment strategy and return expectations accordingly. This is critically important because if your investments don't match your risk tolerance, it will be difficult to combat those times when your emotions want to take over and cause you to act out of fear or panic.

Market risk is the kind of risk that people first think of when it comes to investing, but there are other types of risk, too.

Interest Rate Risk: This is the risk you face when you own an investment paying a certain interest rate and new investments become available at a higher rate. For example, say you just invested in something paying 3% interest. Tomorrow, that same investment is paying 4%. No one wants your investment when they can buy a new one at a higher rate. Accordingly, what you own goes down in value. Interest rate risk is especially applicable to bonds. Interest rates and bonds have an inverse relationship, meaning that as rates rise, bond values fall. We'll talk more about bonds in a bit.

Inflation Risk: Inflation has the effect of reducing the purchasing power of your dollars over time. According to the U.S. Department of Labor, the average annual rate of inflation since 1914 has been approximately 3%. At 3% annual inflation, something that costs $100 today would cost $181 in 20 years. Inflation risk is probably the most overlooked type of risk because it's "invisible." It's not priced every day like a stock. You don't write a check to inflation at the end of the year. Nevertheless, people know that prices rise over time.

Investment Options

There are many, many types of investments and books upon books have been written about them. Generally, for our discussion, they can be classified as either a financial asset or physical asset. A financial asset is a **contractual claim** on something else and takes the form of a piece of paper. On the other hand, physical assets are tangible things like real estate, art and commodities — things you can touch.

Financial Assets

Here is an overview of the various types of financial assets.

Bank Accounts: We covered these earlier. I'm mentioning them again because they are the most fundamental type of financial assets. For money you are going to use in the short term (within the next one to two years), keep that in the bank. When interest rates are low, it may seem foolish to keep money in a bank account that's earning virtually nothing. Get over it. It's just the price you pay for having access to the money. These are funds that you can't risk having the value go down. This is true of your Emergency, Car and Vacation Funds that we spoke about earlier.

Certificates of Deposit (CDs): If you don't need your money in the short term, you might want to invest it somewhere with the opportunity for a higher rate. For example, you might buy a CD that pays you more than your savings account but less than other investments. The longer the timeframe until you need the money, the higher the rate the bank will pay you. The trade-off is the limited access you'll have to your money. You commit to leaving your money untouched for the stated period. So a 3-month CD will usually pay more than a savings account. In turn, a 6-month CD will pay more than the 3-month variety. A 9-month CD will pay more than the 6-month, and so on. If you're willing to commit your money for a longer period, the financial institution you use will typically pay you a higher rate. Be mindful that many banks will charge you a penalty if you withdraw your money before the stated term ends (that is, before the CD matures).

You might decide to use a CD for your Car or Vacation Fund. If you plan to make a purchase next year, a 12-month CD is a way to earn a slightly higher interest rate. It's also a way to "save you from yourself." That is, if the Vacation Fund money is in your bank savings or checking account, it's easier to spend than a CD. CDs are very safe because they are issued by banks and are **FDIC-insured.** This means that if the bank goes out of business, the Federal Deposit Insurance Corporation will step in and pay you back.[34]

Bonds: Governments and companies often issue bonds to finance their activities. When you buy a bond, you are loaning money to the issuing company or government. They agree to pay the money back to you at a future date (the "maturity date") and pay you interest along the way. All things being equal, the further away the maturity date, the higher the interest rate, just like CDs. The amount of interest is stated on the bond. This is also called the **coupon rate.** Bonds are usually purchased in $10,000 increments.

Bonds are considered riskier than CDs but safer than other investments because bondholders are among the first people to be paid if the government or company runs into financial difficulty. Government bonds are considered less risky than corporate bonds because of the

---

[34] FDIC insurance is limited to $250,000 per bank. If you have more than $250,000 that you want to keep in checking, savings and CDs at a bank, it's best to spread it around between different banks.

government's omnipotent authority to raise taxes to satisfy its obligations. You can also buy bond insurance to reduce the risk even further. If something happens to the government issuing the bond, the insurance company will step in and pay the bondholders. Government bonds are issued to fund projects like roads and bridges, and water and sewer authorities. The Federal Government issues bonds, as do states, cities and municipalities.

Corporate bonds aren't considered as safe as government bonds because corporations don't have taxing authority nor is there any bond insurance available for them. In general, the riskiness of a corporate bond depends on the size and financial health of the company. A large profitable company's bonds are considered less risky than those of a small company that is struggling financially. Accordingly, the former will pay a lower coupon rate than the latter since the bondholders must be compensated for taking on more risk. There are also "high yield" bonds, familiarly known as **junk bonds.** These are the riskiest bonds that the average investor should consider. They pay a higher interest rate than other bonds because they can go down in value and are never insured.

Bonds are rated by independent companies to inform investors about the financial strength of the organizations issuing the bonds. The rating scale is a little more complex than the grades you received in school, but the idea is the same: A-rated bonds are considered safer than C-rated bonds. Triple A bonds (AAA) are considered safer than Double A (AA) which are considered safer than Single A and on down the alphabet. Three different companies issue bond ratings: Moody's, S&P and Fitch. Here's an example of ratings and what they mean:

Rating	Definition
AAA, AA and A	High quality, maximum safety
BBB+, BBB and BBB-	Investment grade
BB+	Non-investment grade
BB, BB-	Speculative
B+, B and B-	Highly speculative
CCC+, CCC and CCC-	Substantial risk, in poor standing
DDD, DD and D	Default, issuer may not meet its obligations to investors

Bonds rated BBB or higher are considered "investment grade." This
means that they are conservative bonds suitable for banks and institutions
that need to protect the principal of their investments. They have
obligations to satisfy and don't want to take the risk that their bonds
aren't going to be paid. CCC-rated bonds are considered high yield,
or junk. Bonds and CDs are referred to as **fixed income investments**
because the interest they earn doesn't change; it is a stated percentage.
Common Stocks. Unlike bonds, common stocks don't have coupon rates
or maturity dates, and the common **stockholders** are the last people to
be paid back if the company has financial difficulties. Stocks represent
ownership of a company and you share in its success and failure. When
stocks were originally issued, investors received stock certificates. For
example, you might buy 100 shares of Ford Motor Company. You would
receive a piece of paper stating that you have a claim against the company.
This illustrates that it is a financial asset. Ford doesn't send you a steering
wheel (a physical asset).

Investors buy stocks – often called **equities** – hoping that they grow
in value or "appreciate." This is the time-honored wisdom of "buy low, sell
high." Many stocks also pay **dividends.** This is when a company pays out
a certain amount of its earnings to reward investors for holding its stock.
Dividends are typically paid quarterly and are calculated on a per share basis.

Bonds and stocks are considered **marketable securities.** This just means that there are easily accessible places to buy and sell them, referred to as markets or exchanges. However, although they can be easily bought and sold, there is no promise or guarantee that you will get back the exact amount of your original investment. Hopefully, you'll get back more (a **profit** or **gain)** but you might get back less (a **loss**), sometimes a lot less or even nothing.

Physical Assets

Unlike financial assets, physical assets are not considered to be readily marketable. This is because they are not uniform and there is no easy way for the average investor to price and sell them. Also called **hard assets,** they are considered investments that will protect you against inflation. When you buy 100 shares of Ford Motor Company common stock, your 100 shares are the same as everyone else's 100 shares and you can find the value of your shares on several different websites anytime. This is not the same with art, real estate or commodities. Let's look at these in more detail.

Art: It's obvious that all art is unique; there is no public market where every piece of art is priced every moment of the day. Rather, beauty is in the eye of the beholder and the value is determined by a willing buyer and a willing seller on the day of the transaction.

Investment Real Estate: Like art, every piece of land is unique. Moreover, there are many ways to develop it, if it's developed at all. For example, an investor might buy raw land whose use is not yet determined. Raw land is one of the riskiest ways to invest in real estate because it is unknown if its intended use will come to fruition. At the other end of the real estate investing spectrum are existing properties like shopping malls, office buildings and apartments. Their uses have already been determined but they have their own risks, like whether the tenants continue to pay their rent. The average investor doesn't have the resources to develop raw land or buy a shopping mall, but they might be able to buy a local property or two. This is a more hands-on approach to owning real estate, as you are the owner of the property with the potential for **appreciation** and income. However, you also have the responsibility for managing the tenants, maintaining the property, paying the taxes and collecting the rents directly. Keep in mind that residential real estate is not necessarily a yellow brick road to riches. There was a period between 2000 and 2007 when any kind of real estate increased in value, no matter what it was. People could buy a home one year and sell it the next (called "flipping") with a profit practically guaranteed. But those years were an aberration and are long gone. People still flip houses but these days it involves buying a house that needs improvements of some kind. The amount of work involved in upgrading the property varies from house to house. You don't usually make money just by owning the property for a year.

Commodities like gold, oil and oranges: There are many kinds of **commodities** but for the most part, investing in them is too aggressive for the average person. The price fluctuation and the complexity of purchasing them are better suited to the experienced investor.

Cars and Boats: Physical assets but NOT investments: Don't fool yourself that a car is an investment. Once you drive it off the lot, it is worth less than what you just paid for it. The only time a car is an investment is when it's a "classic" like a 1965 Ford Mustang. The only way not to lose money on cars is to drive them until they die. Think at least 10 years and at least 100,000 miles. Boats are "holes in the water you pour money into." Boats cost a lot of money in gas, maintenance and storage. If you like boating, make friends with people who have boats. Go out with them and drop $100 on party supplies or gas. You'll be a considerate friend and look like a big spender, but you won't own the boat and all its headaches.

Investment Philosophies: Active and Passive

Regardless of what investments you buy, there are the two main ways in which people manage their holdings. **Active management** is when you regularly buy and sell in an effort to maximize your returns. **Passive management** is also referred to as "buy and hold" and that's just what it means. You buy an investment and hold onto it for a long time. Both strategies can be profitable. They are not mutually exclusive and there is no right or wrong choice.

Diversification and Asset Allocation

When it comes to investing, a super important term to know is **diversification,** which essentially means "don't put all of your royal eggs in one basket." It's an almost universally accepted concept that any portfolio should include a mix of investments with varying levels of market risk, interest rate risk, and inflation risk. (NOTE: Diversification does not ensure a profit or guarantee against the possibility of loss.)

Investors who concentrate a sizeable share of their assets in any single investment are courting trouble. Sometimes this happens when people have success with a particular investment and want to own even more of it. Sometimes people make this mistake because they invest heavily in the company where they work. This is particularly risky since their livelihood is also tied to the company's success. That's not to say you shouldn't own company stock; it just means that it shouldn't be all you own — not by a long shot.

Asset allocation is the term for putting together a combination of the different assets that makes sense for your goals and risk tolerance level. Since different assets respond differently to the same news, your stocks may go up while your bonds go down. Many resources are available to assist you in determining how to allocate your assets, including questionnaires to help you match your risk tolerance with sample allocation models. (I've included one in Appendix II.) Ultimately, though, you'll want to choose a mix of investments that has the potential to provide the return you want at the level of risk with which you feel comfortable. A collection of different investments isn't the same as a strategically diversified portfolio. You might own a bunch of great stocks, but if they are all in large US corporations, that's not diverse and it may not be consistent with your goals. Plus, you're overlooking other important assets such as smaller companies, international markets and bonds. Simply put, the average investor diversifies via her asset allocation amongst cash, stocks and bonds.

Funds: Mutual and Exchange Traded

Some say that **mutual funds** are the best investment invention ever. They give the small investor diversification with a small amount of money.

Anyone can buy mutual funds that invest in virtually all of the types of assets that we've covered so far, such as U.S. stocks, international stocks, government bonds and corporate bonds. If you invest something as small as $25 in just one mutual fund, you get to own a small piece of hundreds of companies.

Before mutual funds were invented, investors had to buy shares of each company separately and usually in much larger denominations than $25. Historically, individual stocks were bought in 100-share lots — meaning that, at a minimum, you'd have to buy 100 shares of a stock. If you could only afford to buy 100 shares of one company, that's a lot of risk, as it would be a case of having all your eggs in that one basket. To reduce your risk, you would need to buy 100 shares of several different companies and that's just not practical for most investors – hence, the invention of mutual funds. Mutual funds provide a lot of diversity in a single investment. This is a situation where less is more. Essentially, when you buy a mutual fund, you are pooling your money with other investors.

As a very simple example, let's assume Ann, Beth and Carol each invests $1,000 in XYZ Mutual Fund. By pooling their money, they can buy more than one stock in their fund. Instead of Ann owning ONLY Company A, Beth owning ONLY Company B and Carol owning ONLY Company C, in the mutual fund they each own a bit of Companies A, B and C. So they each reduce their risk of one company having financial difficulty and having their entire investment wiped out. In the real world, mutual funds own hundreds of companies' stocks and bonds, so the risk you have to any one company is reduced dramatically.

In addition to enabling you to invest a small amount of money to own a little bit of a lot of companies, mutual funds:
- Handle the logistics of buying and selling individual stocks and bonds. Even if you have enough money to buy individual stocks to get the diversification you need, the process of buying and selling individual stocks and tracking the number of shares and their performance takes a lot more time than the average person is interested in spending.
- Benefit from "buying power." Because mutual funds invest

enormous amounts of money, they can pay less in transaction costs than an individual investor pays simply because of the volume of shares they buy. Think of this as a volume discount that mutual funds get.

- Calculate the mutual fund's **total return.** There are sophisticated equations to determine how much the investors receive over different timeframes. Mutual funds are required to report their performance over 1-, 3-, 5- and 10-year intervals. Most also provide daily and monthly values, as well as how the fund's done since its inception.

- Allow you to automatically buy and sell shares at any time. You can set up a plan to invest on a regular basis by linking your bank account to the mutual fund. For example, you might invest $25 on the 10th and 25th of every month. All it takes is a phone call to the mutual fund company to sell your shares. You can usually make transactions online, too. Investing the same dollar amount on a regular basis is a strategy called **dollar cost averaging.** This allows you to buy more shares of the mutual fund when its price is low and fewer shares when its price is high.

- Distribute or reinvest dividends. Investors can decide whether to take their distributions in cash or instead use them to buy more shares of the fund.

Exchange traded funds, or ETFs, are a new and improved version of mutual funds. They have lower expenses and give the investor a better way to control tax ramifications than mutual funds do. They are a rapidly growing product in the financial services industry; however, for now, mutual funds comprise 90% of the fund market and remain the dominant choice for diversification.

Mutual funds and ETFs employ the active and passive strategies, too. Active funds buy and sell stocks regularly based on the decisions of the mutual funds' management. These funds have transaction costs involved in buying and selling; plus, they must pay the management team who makes the decisions on what to buy and sell. They earn their fees because they do all the research for you. Evaluating companies and

industries, financial statements, governmental reports and regulations is
a full-time job. The research involved is difficult and time consuming, as
there are more than 25,000 separate stocks and hundreds of thousands of
bonds. A mutual fund has the capacity to analyze and evaluate immense
amounts of data with a depth of resources that individual investors
just don't have. When you buy an actively managed mutual fund, you
delegate this work to the fund company in exchange for a fee. Of course,
fees can reduce your total return, but there are mutual fund managers
who outperform their peers and it makes sense to pay the extra costs for
their skills.

Passive funds, on the other hand, buy a specific group of stocks
that doesn't change. Passive funds have lower expenses because they don't
have the transaction charges that active funds have and they don't need a
management team to buy and sell regularly. They are often called **index**
funds because they might buy all the stocks represented in a specific
index. Indices are indicators and, in finance, refer to a statistical measure
of changes in securities markets. Stock and bond market indices consist
of a hypothetical portfolio representing a particular market or a segment
of it. The most common indices are the **Dow Jones Industrial Average**
(aka, "the Dow") the **S&P 500** and the **NASDAQ;** however, there are
hundreds of indices.

Total Return and Yield

Total return is how investors evaluate the performance of their
investments. It is the sum of the income an investment pays plus the
amount it appreciates in value. Let's say you buy a share of stock in ABC
Company for $10. Over time, each share you purchased appreciates by
$1. You also receive an annual dividend of 5 cents. So, your total return
= the sum of $1 + .05 = $1.05 per share. To calculate the percentage
return, add your initial investment plus the total return. Then divide by
your original investment. Subtract 1. The calculation looks like this: Total
return on ABC company = (($10 + 1.05)/$10) - 1. This equals 0.105. As
a percentage, it equals 10.5%.

In this example, you made money on your investment in ABC,

but this could have gone the other way and you could have lost money. Let's say that you bought each share for $10, the value drops to $9 and you didn't earn any dividends. Following the above formula: Total return on ABC = (($10-1)/$10) – 1. This equals -0.10. As a percentage, it equals -10%.

Since you lost $1 for each of your 100 shares, your total loss = $100. Now your investment is worth only $900 compared to your original $1,000 investment.

Yield is the amount of income your investment generates in interest or dividends relative to its current price. Many times, the interest rate equals the yield. This is true of a savings account or certificate of deposit where the value of your investment doesn't fluctuate; however, the yield of bonds and stocks can vary. For example, let's say you buy a bond for $10,000 with a 5% coupon rate. You receive $500 of interest annually ($10,000 x 0.05 = $500). As long as your bond is worth $10,000, the interest rate equals the yield. Now let's assume the value of the bond decreases to $9,000. You still receive $500 per year, but at $9,000, your yield increases to 5.6% ($500/$9,000 = 0.056). The same calculation can be done for stock dividends. Let's say you bought a share of stock for $10. You receive a $0.50 dividend, so your stock is yielding 5% ($0.50/$10). Even if your stock decreases from $10 to $9 per share, you'll still receive $0.50 per share, but your yield will increase to 5.6% ($0.50/$9 = .056).

Measuring Investment Performance

Primarily, your investment performance should be evaluated based on how you are doing relative to your unique goals. Additionally, you can measure how your investments are performing by comparing them to an **index**. If you're evaluating your portfolio in this way, make sure you are judging your performance against the most appropriate index so that it's an apples-to-apples comparison.

Guard Against Greed and Fear

A strategic investment allocation will help you defeat any emotional dragons. Greed takes over when you're wishing you owned more of the best performing investments at the moment. Fear rears its ugly head when markets are volatile and people are projecting the end of the realm . . . er, world. When you feel either of these emotions take hold, remind yourself that you allocated your assets in a thoughtful and strategic manner to meet your goals and then stick to your plan.

Beware of the Braggarts

Braggarts can be more dangerous than wicked witches. Many people assume that just because someone's said she's made great investments that she has. Well, maybe she has. Maybe she hasn't. You don't know and it doesn't matter anyway. Your investments need to be compatible with your goals and no one else's. Some boast that they own a stock that's performed well over the years, but your rate of return on an investment depends on when you bought it and the price you paid. For example, buying Apple stock in 2017 is a whole lot different than having bought it in the 1980s and riding the wave up.

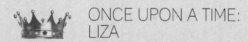

ONCE UPON A TIME:
LIZA

Liza learned the hard way about the risk of having all her investment eggs in one basket. Unfortunately, her dad – and their family – suffered from having too much faith in his company. An executive at one of the largest U.S. auto manufacturers, no one ever thought it would face financial difficulty such that its very existence came into question. With his job and his retirement plan invested all in his company, their whole family's financial future was at risk.

Liza knew about the concept of diversification so she invested in mutual funds and her net worth began to grow. Upon closer examination, though, all the funds Liza bought were invested in large American companies. Although she owned five different funds, they were all buying a lot of the same stocks, so Liza didn't have a lot of diversification after all. Once this was brought to her attention, Liza increased her diversification by adding funds that invested in other asset classes, both in the U.S. and abroad. She added medium and small companies. She expanded her portfolio to include overseas markets, both in developed international markets (like Europe, Australia and Asia) and emerging economies (like India and Brazil). To balance that risk, she bought some funds that invested in government and corporate bonds, too.

Liza's story is a perfect illustration of a woman who was better off making her own investments than delegating the decisions to someone else, even the most important man in her life at the time. Her dad was proud of her for educating herself and making much smarter decisions than he had. Even better, she was proud of herself.

KEYS TO THE CASTLE:

- The Rule of 72 and the miracle of compounding illustrate how investments grow over the long term.

- The more fluctuation in the value of your portfolio that you can tolerate, the larger percentage of your money can be in stocks. If you'd like less volatility, have a higher percentage in fixed income assets like bonds.

- Be honest with yourself in determining how much risk you can handle.

Diversification and asset allocation go hand
in hand. You will want to diversify by allocating
your money among different assets.

There are many different financial products and
every person's situation is unique. Make sure
your investments meet your needs, goals and
risk tolerance, and that those are the primary
factors against which you measure performance.

Part Three

HAPPILY EVER AFTER:
SECURING YOUR FINANCIAL FUTURE

Nine

Some Enchanted Evening: Planning for the Long Term, Both Your Wealth and Your Health

If we're lucky, we're going to grow old. As you age gracefully into a senior monarch, you'll want as many options and as much control as possible over both your wealth and your health. This includes saving to enjoy the active years of retirement and providing for the less active ones.

What does happily ever after mean to you? Have you thought about what your later years will look like? If you're going to fall down a rabbit hole, you'll want to make sure you land in your vision of Wonderland. You will want to be financially wealthy and physically healthy, right? Both contribute to a good quality of life.

If you're not yet in your fifties or sixties, you probably aren't sitting around pondering this, but it's never too early to start planning for what's to come. Your definition of "golden years" might be different than what it means to your friends or any prince that might come along. Women live longer than men so our retirement dollars need to stretch farther. As a woman, you're more likely to need long-term care and may possibly face some of your healthcare needs alone (unless your heirs to the throne, if you have them, take care of you, the queen).

Many people are living for the day when they can retire. Many times, though, they haven't done the math on how much it costs to live currently (remember our discussion about budgeting?), let alone how much it might cost to live when they want to stop working. Here's where planning helps. It gives you time to figure out how to prepare for your later years and to evaluate your options for providing what you need to enjoy the fruits of your life's labor. The sooner you figure it out – and the more concrete you are about it – the better off you're going to be.

Your Future Wealth

The first obvious thing that you'll want to plan for is how much money you'll have to live on after you retire. The responsibility for saving for your retirement is yours. The government will help you a little bit in the form of **Social Security benefits,** but the bulk of the money that you're going to live on will have to come from your savings. You can't rely on Aladdin and his magic lamp. Something to note: Investments in the form of retirement accounts are ALWAYS individual accounts; they are never held jointly. As the sole owner of the retirement account, you have the responsibility of making prudent decisions for these funds consistent with your goals, timeframe and risk tolerance level.

Employer-Sponsored Retirement Plans

If you're lucky, your employer will help you with your retirement savings in the form of a company-sponsored plan. These are often referred to as **qualified retirement plans** and are the best ways to start saving because:
- The money is taken right out of your paycheck so you won't be spending it. This is critical! This money never makes its way to your checking account.
- The money is tax-deductible so you don't pay taxes on it in the current year. In that way, contributing to your retirement plan also has a short-term benefit. For example, if your taxable income is $50,000 and you don't contribute to your retirement plan, you owe income tax on the whole $50,000; but if you contribute

$5,000 to your retirement plan, your taxable income is reduced
and you only pay income tax on $45,000 that year.

- The money grows **tax-deferred.** This means that any earnings
aren't taxed as they accumulate. For example, if you contribute
$5,000 to your retirement plan and it earns 10%, or $500,
you don't pay tax on the $500. On the other hand, if you invested
in something that earns 10% but is not in a retirement plan, you
owe tax on the $500 in the current year. Think back to our
concept of compounding. The earnings in your retirement plan
compound year after year. In that way, retirement plan savings are
a mid-term investment goal, too. You don't have to pay tax on
the money until you withdraw it. That's huge! Continuing
the example above, let's say you contribute $5,000 to your
retirement account. That amount is tax-deductible and your
contribution earns $500 that is not taxed. The next year, your
$5,000 + the $500 it earned grows another 10%. Now you've
earned 10% on $5,500, or $550.

NOTE: Even if you're self-employed, you can set up an employer-
sponsored plan. In those cases, you are both the employer *and* employee.

Defined Contribution and Defined Benefit Plans

There is a lot of variability in company-sponsored retirement plans
and the complexity of them is outside the scope of this book, but
fundamentally, there are two kinds of plans: Defined Contribution and
Defined Benefit. Let's take each in turn.

Defined Contribution Plans are just what their name implies: How
much that's *contributed* to the plan is *defined,* either in a dollar value or
as a percentage. As these are by far the most common types of retirement
plans and they are the only kind that give you some control over the
investments, it's useful to go into the types of defined contribution plans
in a little more detail.

- **401(k) and 403(b) plans.** These are very common types of plans;
401(k)s are for companies and 403(b)s are for not-for-profit
institutions like charities and universities. At a minimum, you

can defer money into these plans. You are "deferring" receipt of your money until a later date; that is, when you withdraw it from the retirement plan. The government allows you to defer as much as $18,500/year[35] but your company's plan might have lower limits. Many times, 401(k)s have a matching contribution and a discretionary contribution made to your account by your employer. There is a lot of variability in 401(k) plans. Some allow employees to take loans against their accounts or withdraw funds for personal financial hardships. To learn about the specifics of your plan, ask your HR department for a copy of the Summary Plan Description (aka, SPD).

- **SIMPLE IRAs.** This type of plan is primarily designed for smaller companies. In fact, SIMPLE is an acronym for Savings Incentive Match Plan for Employees of small employers. There are trade-offs for this simplicity – including, but not limited to, lower contribution limits and no availability for loans. Unlike 401(k) plans, the maximum you can contribute is $12,500/year.[36]

- **SEP IRAs.** The only contributions to SEP IRAs are made by the employer and they are discretionary; there are no **salary deferrals** or match opportunities. If your company has a SEP IRA, you will have an account that you manage but the amount that is contributed each year is at the discretion of the employer. It is out of your control (unless you own the company). This type of plan has become less and less popular since the SIMPLE IRA was created.

Many times, your employer will contribute to your retirement account on your behalf. These types of contributions can take the form of a discretionary contribution, a matching contribution, a non-elective contribution, or some combination.

---

[35] Individuals over age 50 can make "catch up" contributions of an additional $6,000 into 401(k) and 403(b) plans for a total of $24,500 in 2018.

[36] Individuals over age 50 are eligible to make "catch-up" contributions of an additional $3,000 into SIMPLE IRAs for a total contribution of $15,500 in 2018.

- **Discretionary contribution:** This is an amount of money your employer might contribute on your behalf. Because it's discretionary, the company isn't required to add money to your account in this way so think of it as more jewels on the crown.
- **Matching contribution.** This is money the company commits to add to your account if you contribute, too. It's a way to encourage you to participate in the plan; for example, you save 3% of your money in the plan and your company puts in 3%. That's a guaranteed 100% return on your investment. The only other place where you might have a chance for that kind of quick return on your money is gambling. That's not investing; it's gambling! Harken back to our Once Upon a Time story of Elizabeth and her employee. Right away, you've doubled your money in an instant without doing anything more than doing what's best for you. You put in money and the company matches the amount. Not all company matches, however, are 100%. At a minimum, you should contribute up to the percentage that will be matched. If you don't, then you're leaving money on the table. If you only add 1%, then the company will only add 1%. That's 2% you could have had but don't.
- **Non-elective contribution.** This is money that the company commits to contributing to your account whether you save any money or not. For 401(k) plans, the minimum non-elective contribution is 3%. For SIMPLE IRAs, it's 2%.

Defined Benefit Plans, commonly called **pensions,** tell you how much money you'll receive once you've retired; that is, what your retirement *benefit* will be. They are very expensive for employers to maintain so they are less and less common; however, if you've got one, don't disregard the value of this increasingly rare employee benefit.

Additional Retirement Savings Options

You're not limited to saving for your golden years only through employer-sponsored retirement plans. You have more options. If you don't have an employer-sponsored plan, open an IRA. If you do have an employer-sponsored plan, open an IRA to supplement it. As you know well by now, when it comes to saving, more is better. You can open IRAs at a bank or investment company; the range of things you can buy in this type of account is very broad and includes all of the things we've discussed so far.

IRAs: Traditional and Roth

IRAs are a place where you can save for your future retirement on a tax-favored basis separate from and in addition to (as mentioned above) any employer-sponsored plan. There are two kinds:

- **Traditional IRAs.** For most people, when you contribute to a Traditional IRA, you are eligible to deduct the contribution on your tax return. This means that you don't pay income tax on that money in the current year. The money in the account grows tax-sheltered until you take it out — typically after you retire. When you withdraw the money, you pay the tax.

- **Roth IRAs.** Contributions to Roth IRAs are not tax-deductible. The money grows tax-sheltered just like traditional IRAs; however, it's not taxed when you withdraw it. The younger you are, the more valuable is the tax-free nature of future withdrawals (see illustration, below). If you start contributing early, it's likely that the growth on your contributions is going to be more than the money you invested. Again, not owing tax on this money when you eventually withdraw it is huge.[37]

The amount that you can contribute each year to a Traditional or Roth IRA is limited by the government. It is based on your income and how you file your taxes. Which one is right for you depends on your unique circumstances.[38]

Regardless of whether you choose a Traditional or Roth, the money is not intended to be withdrawn before age 59.5. Traditional IRAs require that you start taking money out at age 70.5, but Roth IRAs

---

[37] Some 401(k) plans also have a Roth option where your contributions are not tax-deductible in the current year but withdrawals at retirement are tax-free.

[38] The maximum IRA contribution was $5,500 as of this printing in 2018. Individuals age 50 and older can contribute an additional $1,000 known as a "catch-up" contribution.

don't have that requirement. Ideally, you'll want to save the maximum amount allowed every year. Even if you can't contribute the entire $5,500, contribute something. Your goal is to save the maximum. If you can't, at least get started.

Also bear in mind that retirement plan contributions are calculated on an annual basis. If you don't maximize the contribution in the current year, you can't go back and add money. For example, as stated above, the IRA limit for 2018 was $5,500. Let's say you only contributed $2,000 for that year. In 2020, you can't make up the $3,500 difference for 2018.

The Effect of Compounding

Growth of Annual $5,500 Investment

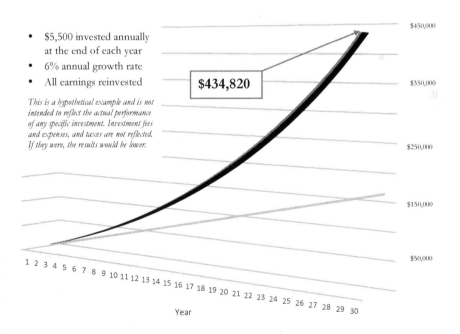

- $5,500 invested annually at the end of each year
- 6% annual growth rate
- All earnings reinvested

This is a hypothetical example and is not intended to reflect the actual performance of any specific investment. Investment fees and expenses, and taxes are not reflected. If they were, the results would be lower.

$434,820

$450,000

$350,000

$250,000

$150,000

$50,000

Year

Annuities

Simply put, an **annuity** is a type of retirement savings vehicle that promises to pay you a certain amount of money for a certain period. Annuities are contracts issued by insurance companies and come in many varieties with different features, benefits, costs and restrictions. After you've put the maximum you can into your employer-sponsored plan and an IRA, you might consider buying an "after-tax annuity" as part of your retirement planning. Although your contributions are not tax-deductible, the earnings grow tax-deferred. When you withdraw the funds later, you'll owe taxes on the growth but not on your original investment. Like other types of retirement accounts, annuities restrict access to the funds until age 59.5. If you take the money out sooner, you'll owe a 10% penalty tax.

Fundamentally, there are two types of annuities:

- Fixed annuities have stated interest rates and detail how much money you'll receive and when. For example, you might buy a $50,000 annuity at age 40. When you retire at age 65, the insurance company promises to pay you $250/month for the rest of your life.

- Variable annuities are much more complex and the amount of money you'll receive depends on how well the variable investments perform. The variable investment options are very similar to mutual funds but are called "sub-accounts." If you invest $50,000 in a variable annuity, you don't know how much the insurance company will pay you; it depends on how your sub-accounts perform over time.

Regardless of the retirement vehicles you use, one of the last things you'll want to do is contribute to your retirement plan but then take the money out before you retire. Reflect back on our earlier discussion of budgeting. It's important that you have a savings account to cover your Emergency Fund and other short- to medium-term expenses like your Vacation and Car Fund. Your retirement savings are not to be used for anything other than retirement. Many plans won't even let you have access to the money before then. If you make a withdrawal, you won't only have to pay income taxes on the money, you'll have to pay a 10% penalty tax, too. That's a very expensive way to pay for things. Plus, it's a slippery slope. Once you take money out of the plan, it's psychologically easier and easier to take more money out in the future. If you start to think of it as a backup Emergency Fund, that's not good. Not good at all.

....

"Snow White is the fairest in the land, but she runs 20 miles a week and spends hours in the gym."

Your Future Health
....

Part of affording your retirement will be maintaining and managing your health as you age. Studies show that 65% of single women without children wonder who will take care of them in their old age.[39] Let's look at this from a positive perspective: Needing long-term care is the benefit you reap from taking care of yourself all your life. Many people are in denial that they will ever need long-term care and that's understandable. No one likes to be infirm and we don't like thinking about it. Most people don't want to be dependent on others. We want to live on our own terms and be completely healthy. Well, again, that's not always reality.

With a decent healthcare regimen, you're going to get old and you probably want the benefits of a long life, if for no other reason than to enjoy the retirement you've been saving for and planning. Technological advances in medicine are miraculous; the longer you live, the greater the chance that doctors can cure most of what ails you. Needing long-term care is part of having the good fortune to get old but at some point, your body is going to break down and you will want to be able to get the care you need.

We don't know the future of healthcare, but what we do know is that most long-term care expenses aren't covered by the biggest retiree healthcare program: Medicare. **Medicare** will pay for some long-term care but it's mostly rehabilitative and requires a hospital stay of at least three days before becoming eligible. And let's face it: no one wants to be in a hospital these days.

As the **Baby Boomers** continue to age, more and more people will face this problem and more solutions will be developed. By the time Gen Xers and Millennials need long-term care, there should be more innovative approaches. For now, though, a very popular strategy is to move into a **continuing care community.**

Continuing care communities provide increasing levels of care as your health declines. For this reason, they are also called "transitional care communities." They can be very luxurious and replicate college campuses with fitness centers, dining options, educational opportunities and social clubs. Able-bodied retirees move to these facilities secure in the knowledge that as they age they won't have to move again; they can "age in place." Once residents can no longer live independently, they then take

[39] "Women Today; New roles, new responsibilities and new financial needs,"Allianz white paper, (2012).

advantage of the assisted living services offered.

Assisted living refers to a whole range of care that might be
needed — from someone coming to your home a few times a week
to help with meals and cleaning to full-time skilled nursing care and
everything in between. It is the most common kind of long-term care.
The goal is to help individuals maintain their independence for as long as
possible. Most people want to stay in their own homes instead of moving
to any kind of facility. Even if they reach a point where they need help
with activities of daily living, like bathing or making sure they take their
medications properly, they can still remain in their residences with help
from in-home care workers. Unless you're very low income (which is not
our goal here, right?), you'll have to pay for these services.

If you live in any kind of metropolitan region, there are probably
services available. Tracking them down and managing them can take an
enormous amount of time. This is something else you probably don't want
to burden your kids with. What if you don't have children? The decline
in your health might be gradual at first then accelerate as you get older.
Eventually, you might find yourself in need of skilled care for a condition
that is debilitating if not critical – things like memory issues, dementia or
Alzheimer's. The more care you need, the more costly it will be.

Long-Term Care Insurance

So how will you pay for any and all of the above? Yep, there's insurance
for that. Long-term care insurance policies are very complex and the
variations of coverage are vast. For our purposes here, these are the things
you will need to consider:

Qualifying for benefits: Most policies begin to provide benefits once you
are no longer able to do two of the six **activities of daily living** (ADLs.)
They are:

1. Eating
2. Bathing
3. Dressing
4. Toileting
5. Transferring

6. Continence

Essentially, there are three components to a long-term care policy: when it starts, how much it pays and how long it pays.

- **Elimination Period:** This is the period you will pay your own expenses before the insurance carrier starts to provide any money toward your care. It is similar to the deductible for car insurance only it is time-based. The shorter the elimination period, the higher your premiums. Your choices range from 30 days to 60, 90, 120 and 180 days. Think about coordinating this with your Emergency Fund.

- **Benefit Amount:** This is the dollar value that the insurance carrier will pay you. Sometimes it is expressed as a daily amount; other times, it is a monthly number. For example, one policy might cover you for $200/day and another might be $6,000/month.

- **Benefit Period:** This is the length of time that the insurance carrier will pay a benefit to you. For example, if you select a benefit period of 4 years at $200/day, the maximum the insurance company will pay is $292,000 (= 365 x 4 x $200).

When deciding on long-term care insurance, you will want to work with a qualified agent with a reputable carrier and discuss all the options and risks. She can craft a policy to meet your budget and goals. It's almost impossible to get up to speed quickly – or to stay current – on long-term care insurance on your own. Policy terms are always changing and insurance companies have gotten in and out of the business over the last few decades.

Most people balk at the high cost of long-term care insurance. Well, it costs a lot because the chances are high you're going to access some of the benefits. What if you don't? What if you never use it? What if you die a sudden death (as most people want) and never access the benefits? Well, as I've pointed out earlier, it's insurance, so you don't want to collect the benefit. On the other hand, you want to realize some of the value you've paid into it.

Fortunately, insurance carriers are developing new products to address these issues. Some are marrying life insurance policies with long-term care coverage. As a life insurance policy, there is a death benefit; however, there is also a long-term care feature attached to the policy so that you can

access funds for the care you need. The more money you withdraw from
the policy for healthcare, the less death benefit is left. Either way, you realize
some benefit from the premiums you pay.

Some of these policies are structured as a "single premium" with the
idea that you "invest" a large sum of money and then can access some multiple
of that in long-term care benefits. For example, you might make a premium
payment of $50,000 that allows you to withdraw $250,000 of long-term
care benefits over some period. If you die before accessing the long-term care
benefits, the $50,000 premium instead pays a death benefit of $300,000.

Foregoing Long-Term Care Insurance

You might be wondering: *What if I don't opt to get long-term care insurance?
What other options do I have for my care?* Ideally, you'll be in a position where
you have enough money to pay for any care that you need. If you don't have
enough money to pay for your care, then maybe your family does. Maybe they
can all chip in to cover the costs of any care you need or buy the long-term care
insurance policy on your behalf.

If you're married, you and your spouse can care for one another. The
big expenses come, though, when one spouse can live independently and the
other requires skilled care in a facility. In that situation, you end up paying the
costs of two households. Maybe you can move in with one of your children.
Almost all parents I know don't want to do that. We don't want to be a burden
to our children and we don't necessarily want to live with them.

What to do if you're single? How about talking to your friends about
their plans? Maybe you can put together a transitional living situation until
care is needed. Maybe you share a house with a couple of other women. You
can each have your own space with the benefit of not being alone. These can be
very fluid co-housing situations where you share costs but aren't required to be
together 24/7. You might think of it like people use a beach house with friends.
You share the costs. You can spend time together or you can go your own way.

This is not common – yet – but it's certainly something to consider
and is happening in communities around the country. It's a viable model
whether you live in a city or out in the country. In fact, it might be more
viable out in suburbia or exurbia since people tend not to be as close with their
neighbors as those who live in proximity.

ONCE UPON A TIME:
CHELSEA

Chelsea, 30, is an accountant for a local firm and her career is progressing just as she'd hoped. Chelsea is excited about her career prospects. She expects that in the future, she'll want to enjoy the fruits of her labor and retire with a nice financial cushion. Her job is a demanding one, especially during tax time, but she's on track to being a partner and believes she'll have more control over the number of hours she has to work when that happens. In the meantime, she and her husband are doing their best to balance their work, marriage and their kids' schedules.

Chelsea's mother always advised her to "begin with the end in mind." She was fortunate in that her first boss told her the first thing she should do is begin saving into the company's retirement plan. Since this money is automatically deducted from her paycheck, she doesn't miss it. With time on her side, this money has the opportunity to grow significantly. Moreover, that same timeframe will work to Chelsea's advantage in the amount of risk she can take.

Although not an investment advisor, her boss recommended that she consider a **target date fund.** This type of fund matches the investments in the fund with the year you plan to retire. The closer you get to retirement and the sooner you'll need the money, the more conservative the fund becomes. (Target date funds are a mix of mutual funds that invest in different kinds of stocks and bonds. They provide a lot of diversification with a small amount of money.)

Sadly, Chelsea's dad passed away a few years ago. The good news for him is that it was sudden and painless. The bad news is that Chelsea's mom was recently diagnosed with early onset Alzheimer's disease. With her dad gone,

the responsibility for her mom's care has become Chelsea's.
Chelsea knows that her mom bought a long-term care
insurance policy years ago but she doesn't know anything
about it. She figured that there's no time like the present to
learn the details.

Chelsea contacted her parent's insurance agent and
learned that her mom's policy has a 90-day elimination period
with a $6,000 per month benefit and a four-year benefit
period. Since Chelsea's mom can no longer feed or bathe
herself, on January 1, Chelsea and the agent contacted the
insurance company to advise them of her mom's current health
and to learn how to proceed. Her mom had to pay the cost
of any care she needed from January 1 through March 31
(90 days.) On April 1, she became eligible to receive benefits.
Going forward, the insurance carrier will pay $6,000 per
month toward Chelsea's mom's care for four years. At that
point, the insurance company will have provided $288,000 in
benefits ($6,000/month for 48 months). After that, Chelsea's
mom again becomes responsible for all costs.

Chelsea is grateful that she can be with her mom at
this time in her life. Nevertheless, it has taken a toll on her
emotionally and physically. This carried over to her husband
and children, as well as her work. Thankfully, Chelsea's boss
was very understanding of her situation. She'd gone through
something similar with her own parents, but what would
Chelsea have done if she wasn't so empathetic? Chelsea knows
that she doesn't want to put her own kids through what she's
going through even if they can and want to care for her. She
doesn't like thinking about it, but now she's motivated to get
long-term care insurance for herself and her husband.

KEYS TO THE CASTLE:

- Envision what your retirement dreams look like. These are personal and might be different than your friends' and family's

- Remember that your retirement is your responsibility.

- Participate in any company-sponsored retirement plan as soon as you are eligible and, at a minimum, defer enough of your salary to receive the maximum match the company makes on your behalf.

- After maximizing your company-sponsored plan, put as much money as you can into an IRA each calendar year.

- Accept that as you age you'll probably need help caring for yourself.

- Investigate the different types of care where you live to get a sense of the range of costs.

Ten
Protecting the Royal Blood Line: Important Life Documents

The task of "getting your affairs in order" doesn't have to be morbid or depressing. Think about it as protecting the royal bloodline — yours and that of your heirs. Together, all of the following documents comprise your estate plan. If you don't make these decisions, someone else will make them for you.

Depending on your life situation, an estate plan might be as simple as making sure that the people you list as beneficiaries on your life insurance and retirement plans are current. However, if you've accumulated any assets in your own name, you'll need a **will.** If you have children, you'll need a will even if you don't have assets. So, let's talk about this important document first.

Will

A will is the first (and sometimes only) document that comes to mind when creating an estate plan. If there's a will, there's a way, right? What's a will? In simple terms, it's just your way of being in control of who gets your stuff once you don't need it anymore. It's also an opportunity for you to make charitable gifts to organizations that are important to you. If you don't tell people what you want to do with your assets, then they'll decide without you – or the laws in the state where you live will dictate what happens. You don't want that. Nobody wants that. As the reigning queen of your own life, you'll want to rule over these decisions, too. And remember, you can change your mind at any time and update the document.

People are grieving when a loved one passes away. If there are children involved, everyone wants to do what's in the best interest of the children. Yet it's possible – if not likely – that not everyone is going to agree on this and you don't want someone else calling the shots. Many times, parents don't write their wills because they can't decide on – or agree on – a **guardian** for their children. Keep in mind that you are the ideal people to raise your children; everyone else is a distant second. That almost makes it more important for you to make the decision. You'll want to choose who is the best of the bunch. Then you need to confirm that they're willing to take on the responsibility, as it's not one to be taken lightly. If you think your choice might hurt some feelings, then keep a letter explaining your reasoning and the conclusion you've reached. Writing your will and determining the disposition of your children – your most important asset – is too important to leave to fate just because you think someone's feelings might be hurt.

Some people don't write their wills because they are superstitious. They think that as soon as they do, they'll be struck by lightning or hit by a bus. Of course, this is silly. I get it, though. No one wants to spend money on a lawyer to talk about their demise, but if you've got assets and/or children, get thee to an attorney. Dying is a part of life. Having this important document will give you peace of mind and is a huge gift to your loved ones. Don't abdicate this responsibility.

Again, keep in mind that you can change your will whenever and as many times as you want. It's not carved in stone. It's written on paper and can be updated when things change — and things are going to change. You're going to be accumulating more assets over the decades so your situation is going to get more complex. If you've got kids, they are going to grow up and at a certain point they won't need a guardian anymore. You might have grandchildren and that might affect your thinking about who gets what. Aside from your personal situation, tax laws change frequently and, many times, they affect this type of planning. So, you'll need to revisit your will at least every five years – sooner if some life event occurs or the tax law changes.

Writing Your Own Will

Yes, it's okay to write your own will. You can go online and use a cheap template. (Just Google "will template.") But don't underestimate the value of the advice of an expert. Laws in this area vary by state, so what's an appropriate strategy for you in New York might not be the same for your friend in New Mexico. This is a situation where you don't know what you don't know and it's important to get it right. Also, don't undervalue your time. Spending it studying the laws of your state might not be the best use of it. Plus, a lawyer can tell you what will happen if you don't write your will and that might be enough to shock you into action!

Naming an Executor

Part of the process of writing a will is naming an **executor,** also known as an administrator. This is the person who makes sure the directions in the will are carried out. This individual should probably be a resident of your state, as it just makes it easier to get things done. Keep in mind that you're not doing anyone a favor by asking her to be the executor since it takes some time to sort things out. For this reason, your will can express that the executor be compensated for her time.

It will probably be easiest for them to work with an attorney, too. Getting current on the laws of administering the will is probably not a good use of their time, either. Sometimes, children can get bent out of shape if they think their parents are favoring one child over the other when selecting an executor. Long-term, dysfunctional family dynamics can rear its ugly head, but the fact is that someone has to handle things and parents are doing their best just like everyone else.

Not all assets will pass through your will. Essentially, there are three ways that your assets can be transferred when you die:
- **By will.** These are the assets that you own solely in your name and will be distributed according to your will.
- **By joint ownership.** These are the things that you co-own with someone else. If something happens to you, the asset becomes the property of the remaining owners.
- **By beneficiary.** These are assets for which you name a beneficiary;

they are most commonly retirement accounts and life insurance. If something happens to you, they are paid directly to the beneficiary.

Each of these three is separate and independent of the other. For example, you might change the heirs in your will, but that won't automatically change the beneficiary on your life insurance. You might state in your will that you want your house to pass directly to your children from your first marriage, but if you own it jointly with your second husband, it will pass to him. Being joint owners means that the account will NOT pass through your will; it will pass directly to the other owner(s).

Power of Attorney

A financial or property **power of attorney** (POA) document gives someone you trust the power to act on your behalf. They can access your bank accounts, make investment decisions, and essentially handle all the duties related to your assets. Having someone's power of attorney is a fiduciary obligation, meaning that the person with the POA must act in the best interest of the person who gave it to her and not in her own self-interest.

There are two types of POAs: durable and springing. The durable one is preferable in that someone can act of your behalf as soon as necessary. A springing POA requires a court order determining you to be incompetent to act on your own affairs. It doesn't "spring" into action until then – hence, its name. NOTE: A POA ends when you die. Upon your passing, the executor takes over in managing your assets, which at that point are part of your estate.

Medical Directive and Medical Power of Attorney

The former tells everyone what you want to have happen if you're seriously ill; the latter gives someone the power to make sure that what you want to have happen happens. These documents are helpful to everyone who may be involved in your medical care. In situations like this, you don't want someone else making the call about your healthcare. Writing these papers doesn't have to be complicated; just state clearly what you want to have done and what you don't. End of story.

ONCE UPON A TIME: GRACE

In the prime of her life, Grace was in good health with a loving family and an engaging career. She loved to travel and had gone to the Galapagos Islands, Antarctica and on African safari.

Sadly, in her mid-forties, Grace was diagnosed with Lou Gehrig's disease. Although her mind was sound, her physical health deteriorated rapidly. Having never written a will prior to the onset of the disease, Grace spent the last six months of her life scrambling to get her financial affairs in order and trying to put together her estate plan. In the end, she did have enough time to address 90% of the issues she needed to face. Unfortunately, doing so came at the expense of not being able to spend her last days focusing on quality time with her family and other loved ones.

KEYS TO THE CASTLE:

- Get a will. This is the foundation of any estate plan.

- Make sure your beneficiary designations are up to date. Remember that assets that pass by beneficiary do not go through your will.

- Designate a power of attorney to act on your behalf for your financial matters.

- Have a medical directive and medical power of attorney so that someone knows what kind of medical care you want and don't want and can make sure your wishes are followed.

Eleven

Fairy Godmother or Financial Advisor?

"Whenever you call, I will help you."

The fairy godmother spoke these words of reassurance to Cinderella. Having a financial advisor that you can call upon can be just as comforting and a bit more practical. And let's face it: You're a busy woman. You may not have the time, interest, inclination or discipline to do your own financial planning. That's okay. There are plenty of people who can help. Yes, you will have to compensate them, just as you would anyone else who provides a professional service. Don't get hung up on this but do be sure that you understand how your financial advisor is paid (more on that in a bit).

So how do you find the right financial advisor? It's not much different than finding the right doctor or lawyer. Start by asking for referrals. You're looking for someone with whom you can communicate. You want them to speak to you respectfully and explain things clearly. As you've seen throughout this book, the financial services industry has its own vocabulary. This is truly one place where there are no stupid questions. It's your money so you need someone to answer your questions to your satisfaction. You may want to support women in the business by seeking out a female advisor. If you do, it might take some searching since only 16% of financial advisors are women.[40]

Services Provided by Financial Professionals

Essentially, you can hire a financial advisor to help with any or all the parts of the financial planning process detailed in these chapters. At a minimum, they will usually:

- Review and prioritize your goals and objectives.
- Review your current investment portfolio and develop an asset management strategy.
- Answer your questions.

Additionally, many will:

- Develop a summary of your current financial situation, including a net worth statement, cash flow summary and insurance coverage.
- Complete a retirement plan assessment, including financial projections of assets required for your estimated retirement date.
- Identify tax-planning strategies to optimize your financial position.
- Present a written financial plan that they will review in detail with you. It will contain recommendations designed to meet your stated goals and objectives, supported by relevant financial summaries.
- Develop an action plan to implement the agreed upon recommendations.
- Assist you with the implementation of the financial plan.
- Monitor the plan and adjust it as needed to match your changing goals and life circumstances.
- Keep current on new legislation and tax changes that may be applicable to your situation.
- Refer you to other professionals like accountants and attorneys to assist with implementation of the action plan.

There is a lot of variety in what advisors provide. Be sure to get an

---

[40] Cerulli Associates, "Only 16% of Advisors Are Women," *Investment Advisor Magazine* (January 18, 2017).

engagement agreement that details the nature and scope of the services, the responsibilities of each party and associated costs.

Compensation Arrangements

Historically, compensation in the financial services business has been a lot of "smoke and mirrors", which has given it a bad reputation. Clients weren't clear on how their advisors got paid and were too uncomfortable asking. Times have changed and transparency is now the industry watchword. In fact, the Financial Planning Association requires its members to be up front with their clients about how they are compensated.

Fees are important because the more you pay, the more it eats into your investment returns; however, this might not be the time to shop solely for the lowest cost provider. You probably don't want someone managing your money on the cheap. In general, there are three ways that financial advisors get paid:

- **Project-based:** If you're hiring someone to address a specific issue like a retirement projection, consider paying a one-time flat fee for the advice or an hourly rate with an upward limit on the total cost. In this type of relationship, you provide the relevant information then the advisor gives you objective recommendations and sends you on your way. There is no ongoing relationship.

- **Commissions:** Advisors compensated by commissions get paid when you buy an insurance or investment product. Also called a sales charge, commissions vary by company and product. Some people believe that paying commissions gives the advisor incentive to **churn** your account. That is, since they only get paid if you buy or sell something, they might be motivated to continually make transactions so that they continue to make money. Not only is this unethical, it's illegal. It's based on the premise that the advisor is putting her interests ahead of your own. This isn't necessarily true, of course. There are plenty of honest, ethical financial advisors working in their clients' best interests that earn commissions.

- **Percentage of invested assets.** Although the insurance industry is still largely commission-based, it is more and more popular for investment advisors to be compensated by a percentage of the money they manage. This is referred to as **fee-based** management. Investors tend to like this as it "puts the advisor on the same side of the table as the client." That is, as the investor's portfolio increases in value, so does the advisor's income. The industry average is 1%, but many firms offer a sliding scale with the percentage declining with the more money you invest.

Some advisors get paid in some combination of the above ways. For example, you might pay a flat fee for a comprehensive financial plan. This compensates the advisor for her time and expertise regardless of whether you implement the plan. It assures you that the recommendations are objective and not skewed to products that the advisor sells. If you and the advisor agree that you need to increase your insurance coverage and you buy the insurance through your advisor, she will probably earn a commission. If you invest your money with her, she might charge you a percentage of the assets she will be managing.

WHAT IF **WONDER WOMAN** WAS A **DISNEY PRINCESS?**

Financial Advisor Qualifications and Certifications

While certifications are not everything, they should be one of the criteria you consider when selecting a financial advisor. Credentials demonstrate commitment to their area of expertise. Many issuing organizations require completion of extensive study and rigorous examinations to obtain the designation. Often, there are ongoing continuing education requirements. This is very important as the financial services industry is always evolving and the tax code and regulations change over time.

Some accrediting institutions require the holders of their designations to adhere to professional standards and to be bound by a code of ethics. Ask if they are held to the **fiduciary** standard — placing your interests ahead of their own. An example is that they must provide you with the best products to meet your needs and not those that might pay them more.

Often called the "alphabet soup", there are dozens of professional designations within the financial services industry. Below are some of the more common ones. Many advisors have more than one designation.

AAMS. Accredited Asset Management Specialist
- Issued by Certified Financial Planner Board of Standards, Inc.
- Provide a comprehensive approach to financial planning covering insurance, estate, retirement, tax, education and investment planning
- Must pass an exam and adhere to a code of ethics
- Continuing education: 16 hours every 2 years

CFP.® CERTIFIED FINANCIAL PLANNER™
- Issued by Certified Financial Planner Board of Standards, Inc.
- Provide a comprehensive approach to financial planning covering insurance, estate, retirement, education, tax and investment planning
- Must pass a 10-hour, 285-question exam, have 3 years of professional experience, a bachelor's degree and adhere to the fiduciary standard
- Continuing education: 30 hours every 2 year

CFS. Certified Fund Specialist
- Issued by the Institute of Business and Finance
- Have expertise in mutual funds and the mutual fund industry
- Must complete a 60-hour self-study program
- Continuing education is not required

CDFA. Certified Divorce Financial Analyst
- Issued by the Institute for Divorce Financial Analysts
- Analyze data and provide expertise on the financial issues of divorce, assisting both the client and her attorney
- Must have 3 years of experience in the financial services field, accounting or family law
- Continuing education: 15 divorce-specific hours every 2 years

CEBS. Certified Employee Benefits Specialist
- Issued by the International Foundation of Employee Benefit Plans in partnership with the Wharton School of the University of Pennsylvania
- Focus on employee compensation and benefits
- Must complete a curriculum consisting of 2 parts: 6 required courses covering the basic tenets of employee benefits and 2 electives to focus on an area of specialization
- Continuing education is not required

CLU. Chartered Life Underwriter
- Issued by the American College of Financial Services
- Comprehensive approach to financial planning with a strong focus on insurance laws and regulations
- Must complete a 10-course program, including insurance, estate, retirement, education, tax and investment planning
- Continuing education: 30 hours every 2 years

ChFC. Chartered Financial Consultant
- Issued by the American College of Financial Services
- Comprehensive approach to financial planning
- Must complete a 10-course program including, insurance, estate, retirement, education, tax and investment planning, and 3 years of experience in the financial industry; a bachelor's degree is not required
- Continuing education: 30 hours every 2 years

CFA. Chartered Financial Analyst
- Issued by the CFA Institute
- Quantitative analysis of economics, financial reporting, security selection, corporate finance and portfolio management
- Must pass 3 rigorous exams, have at least 4 years of work experience, and maintain ethical and professional conduct
- Continuing education is not required

CIMA. Certified Investment Management Analyst
- Issued by the Investment Management Consultants Association
- Focus on asset allocation, due diligence, risk and performance measurement
- Must complete a 2-hour qualification exam, 250 hours of study, a 4-hour completion exam, and have 3 years of professional experience
- Continuing education: 40 hours every 2 years

CPA. Certified Public Accountant
- Issued by the American Institute of Certified Public Accountants (AICPA)
- Provide accounting and business consulting to individuals and companies
- Must pass 6 rigorous exams related to tax, auditing, financial reporting and regulation
- Continuing education: 120 hours every 3 years

CPCU. Chartered Property Casualty Underwriter
- Issued by the American Institute for Chartered Property Casualty Underwriters
- Specialize in risk management, property and casualty insurance
- Must pass 8 national exams on insurance law, accounting, risk management and ethics
- Continuing education is not required

CRPC. Chartered Retirement Planning Counselor
- Issued by the College for Financial Planning
- Focus solely on retirement planning
- Must pass a closed book final exam
- Continuing education: 16 hours every 2 years

EA. Enrolled Agent
- Issued by the Internal Revenue Service
- Empowered to represent taxpayers before the Internal Revenue Service
- Must pass a written exam and have IRS experience
- Continuing education: 72 hours over a 3-year enrollment period

LUTCF. Life Underwriter Training Council Fellow
- Issued jointly by the College for Financial Planning and the National Association of Insurance and Financial Advisors (NAIFA)
- Help to train new insurance agents and advisors with business building and practice management
- Must be a member in good standing with NAIFA and complete 3 9-week courses
- Continuing education: 3 hours of ethics every 2 years

PFS. Personal Financial Specialist
- Issued by the American Institute of Certified Public Accountants
- For CPAs focusing on individual financial planning, not just accounting
- Must have at least 2 years of teaching or business experience in

personal financial planning and a minimum of 75 hours of personal financial planning education
- Required to pass a comprehensive 160-question exam
- Continuing education: 60 hours every 3 years

Registered Representative and Registered Investment Advisory Associates
- Administered by the Financial Industry Regulatory Authority (FINRA)
- Registered Representatives work for a brokerage company and sell investments
  - Series 6 representatives are licensed to sell mutual funds and variable annuities
  - Series 7 representatives can sell mutual funds and variable annuities as well as stocks, bonds, real estate partnerships and most other investment products
  - Series 65 or 66 representatives are Registered Investment Advisory Associates and allowed to charge fees not just sell commission-based products
- Required to pass a written exam for each registration
- Continuing education: annual requirements by both their firms and FINRA

RIA. Registered Investment Advisor
- Issued by either the Securities and Exchange Commission (SEC) or state regulatory authorities depending on the size of the firm
- Provide investment advice and have a fiduciary obligation
- Must pass a written exam for the Series 65 license

If your financial advisor's designation isn't included above, just Google it for the details on how one obtains and maintains the accreditation.

ONCE UPON A TIME: OLIVIA AND AUSTIN

Olivia and Austin have done a great job identifying their goals, managing their income and expenses in the short-term, and planning their financial future. Olivia is an attorney and works for the government while Austin works in sales for a pharmaceutical company. Olivia's income is consistent; she has good benefits and a likely pension if she stays in her current position long enough. She has always worked outside the home, going part-time for a few years when their two children were really little. Although she doesn't have the opportunity for bonuses, she does have regular hours and a lot of vacation time. Austin, on the other hand, travels quite a bit. He can earn a lot of money, but some years are better than others.

Olivia and Austin have the luxury of their parents being in adjoining towns. Although they don't rely on them for daily childcare, they do provide a safety net should anyone's schedule go awry, such as when there's a breakdown in the public transit system or a need to retrieve a sick child from school in the middle of the day.

Olivia and Austin have always been good savers and have accumulated quite a lot of money, but you wouldn't know it by looking at their chosen lifestyle. As Olivia says, their house is the size of some friends' walk-in closets. They are in their late forties and have no mortgage debt. Olivia's car was paid off a few years ago and they just finished paying off Austin's. They drive their modest cars until they "die" – usually about 10 years. Although maintenance can cost a few thousand dollars a year in the later years, they figure that it's still less than spending $25,000+ on a new car.

They've also begun saving for their children's college educations and will be able to afford paying full tuition at a state university for both of them. When the time comes, if one of their kids attends a private college, they'll be a little strapped for a few years, but they understand that and will adjust their lifestyle accordingly.

Olivia's sister, Abby, is a financial advisor and she's helped them stay focused on their goals. Since they "don't know what they don't know", Abby's made sure they've addressed all the items that comprise a sound financial plan. Since she's part of the family, Abby knows when big life events happen that might cause them to adjust course, but she also knows how busy their day-to-day schedules are. Abby makes sure that nothing "falls through the cracks." She follows up with them regularly to confirm their goals and make sure they stay on track for their own version of "happily ever after." In fact, she treats all her clients like members of the royal family.

Olivia and Austin know their way of living isn't for everyone, but they are happy with the choices they've made and proud of the financial success they've achieved.

KEYS TO THE CASTLE:

- Ask your friends for referrals to financial advisors and meet with a few to determine whom you feel most comfortable working with.

- Understand how your financial advisor gets compensated and how it might or might not affect her recommendations.

- Enter into an engagement agreement with the advisor so you know what to expect of the working relationship, including what your responsibilities are and what hers are.

Twelve

Keep Calm and Reign On

So now, you're on your way to ruling your financial landscape. You are armed to slay the biggest dragon facing women and money: a lack of confidence. You have the basics of cash management, loans and interest rates. You've got the fundamentals of insurance, investing and preparing for the long-term – both yours and your heirs. You can do this – either on your own or with some qualified help. You have the power to control your financial future. After all, you're the queen!

TOP 10 RULES FOR YOUR REIGN:

1. Don't abdicate your financial health to anyone else.
2. Set your goals.
3. Learn the numbers – how much you have and how much you spend.
4. Match the amount of money you'll need with when you'll need it.
5. Spend less than you earn and save as much as you can.
6. Evaluate your insurance needs and options to protect your health and your stuff.
7. Make sure your investments are appropriate for you and not someone else.
8. Maximize your retirement plan.
9. Get your affairs in order for the heirs to the throne. Have a will, powers of attorney (legal and medical) and a medical directive.
10. Ask for help when you need it.

Glossary

Yes, the financial industry has its own language. You don't have to go crazy learning all of the terminology, but knowing your way around the territory with some basic knowledge is going to help you tremendously. This list is in no way exhaustive – and if it exhausts you to read it, just refer to it when the need arises.

Active Management: Buying, selling and continuously monitoring investments to exploit profitable conditions.

Activities of Daily Living [ADL]: Six routine activities that people do every day, including eating, bathing, dressing, toileting, transferring and maintaining continence.

Adjustable Life: A permanent insurance policy that allows changes to the amount of the death benefit, premium amount and payment period; aka, universal life or flexible life.

Adjustable Rate: A mortgage or other loan in which the interest rate may change over the term of the loan.

After-Tax: The amount of money left over after all federal, state and withholding taxes have been deducted from your taxable income.

Alimony: Money paid under court order to one spouse from his or her former spouse.

Annuity: An insurance contract that pays out income, typically used as part of a retirement strategy.

Any Occupation Disability: Your inability to work in a job that is reasonably suitable for you based on things such as education, experience and age.

Appreciation: An increase in the value of an asset over time.

Asset: Anything you own that's of value like a bank account, retirement plan, house or car.

Asset Allocation: An investment strategy to apportion a portfolio according to an individual's goals, risk tolerance and investment horizon.

Assisted Living: Housing that combines healthcare and help with activities of daily living and is a step below a nursing home in terms of the level of care provided.

Auto Insurance: Protects against damages or theft of your vehicle, as well as legal responsibility to others for property damage, physical injury and related medical costs.

Baby Boomer: Someone born between 1946 and 1964.

Balance Sheet: A statement of a person or company's assets, liabilities and net worth; also called a statement of financial position.

Beneficiary: Anyone eligible to receive distributions from a will or life insurance policy.

Bond: Investment in which an investor loans money to an entity for a defined period at a stated rate. Used by companies, municipalities, states and sovereign governments to raise money and finance a variety of projects.

Braggart: Someone who boasts about achievements; aka, a blowhard, big talker or windbag.

Budget: An estimation of income and expenses over a specified time.

Cash Flow: The net amount of cash into and out of a household or business.

Cash Value: The savings portion of a permanent life insurance policy.

Churn: Excessive buying and selling by an investment professional solely to generate commissions.

Claim: A formal request to an insurance company to pay for a covered loss.

Collateral: Property or other assets that a borrower offers a lender to secure a loan.

Commission: Service charge assessed by a broker or advisor in return for providing advice and/or handling the purchase or sale of an investment.

Commodities: Basic goods that are interchangeable with others of the same type; for example, gold, lead and corn.

Common Stock: A financial asset that represents ownership in a corporation.

Compound Interest: Interest calculated on the initial principal and the accumulated interest of previous periods. Can be thought of as "interest on interest."

Continuing Care Community: A retirement community that allows residents to transition from independent to assisted living and skilled nursing care.

Contractual Claim: Investment whose value is determined by what it represents; for example, a CD or stock certificate.

Coupon Rate: Interest rate paid to bondholders by the bond issuer.

Credit: The ability to obtain goods and services before payment based on the commitment that payment will be made in the future.

Credit History, Credit Rating, Credit Score, Credit Report: Records of a consumer's ability and demonstrated responsibility in repaying debts.

Crown: A circular ornamental headpiece worn by a monarch as a symbol of authority, usually made of or decorated with precious metals and jewels.

Damsel: Young, unmarried woman commonly in distress.

Death Benefit: The amount of a life insurance policy, annuity or pension that is payable to the beneficiary when the insured or annuitant passes away.

Deductible: The amount of money an individual pays for expenses before her insurance plan starts to pay.

Defined Benefit Plan: A company retirement plan that provides employees with a fixed payment based on length of employment and salary history.

Defined Contribution Plan: A company retirement plan that provides employees and employers with a way to save a specific dollar amount or percentage for their retirement.

Discretionary Expenses: Costs that are not essential, often viewed as "wants" rather than "needs."

Diversification: Reducing risk by allocating money among various types of investments.

Dividends: Distribution of a portion of a company's earnings to its shareholders.

Dollar Cost Averaging: Buying a fixed dollar amount on a regular schedule, regardless of the share price, resulting in purchasing more shares when prices are low and fewer shares when prices are high.

Dow Jones Industrial Average [The Dow]: A stock market index based on the value of 30 large public U.S. companies.

Down Payment: Cash payment made at the beginning of the purchase of an expensive good or service representing only a percentage of the full purchase price.

Dragon: A mythical monster (typically fire-breathing) symbolizing evil that can be slayed with knowledge.

Durable Goods: Products like appliances that are not consumed in use and can be used for a period of time, usually three or more years; for example, a refrigerator.

Emergency Fund or Personal Security Fund: An account in which you set aside money to be used for unexpected expenses.

Engagement Agreement: Written agreement to perform services in exchange for compensation.

Equity: In reference to investing, a share in a company. In reference to a house, the value of the property after all remaining debts are paid.

Essential Expenses: Costs of basic needs like food, housing, clothing and transportation.

Exchange Traded Fund [ETF]: A pool of funds collected from many people to buy a basket of assets like an index fund.

Executor: Individual appointed to administer the estate of a deceased person.

Fairy Tale: A farfetched story or tall tale that is not only not true, but could not possibly be true.

FDIC: Federal Deposit Insurance Corporation, which insures deposits against bank failure.

Fee-based: A compensation arrangement with a financial advisor who charges a flat fee or a percentage of money invested.

Fiduciary: A person or organization that is ethically bound to act in another's best interests.

Financial Asset: An asset that derives value because of a contractual claim of what it represents; for example, stocks, bonds and bank deposits.

Financing: The act of providing money to make a purchase.

FINRA: Financial Industry Regulatory Authority, which governs all business dealings conducted between dealers, brokers and public investors.

Fixed Expenses: Costs that do not change or vary in amount.

Fixed Rate: Interest rate that doesn't fluctuate during the period of a loan or investment.

Flexible Life: A permanent insurance policy that allows changes to the amount of the death benefit, premium amount and payment period; aka, adjustable life or universal life.

Gain: An increase in the value of an asset that gives it a higher worth than the purchase price.

Guardian: Individual given the legal responsibility to care for a child or adult.

Hard Assets: Investments with intrinsic value such as oil, precious metals and real estate.

Health Savings Account [HSA]: For medical expenses not covered by HDHPs. Contributions are tax-deductible and limited to a yearly maximum.

High Deductible Health Plan [HDHP]: Health insurance policy with a deductible of at least $1,300 for an individual and at least $2,600 for a family.

Homeowner's Insurance: Protects against damages to the structure of or possessions in the home.

Human Capital: The economic value of an employee's skill set, including education, experience, work ethic and leadership qualities.

Index: An aggregate value to represent an entire market and track its changes over time.

Inflation: The rate at which the general level of prices for goods and services is rising.

Interest: The price of borrowing or lending money, typically expressed as an annual percentage rate.

Joint Tenants With Rights of Survivorship [JTWROS]: A type of ownership in which all owners have equal portions of ownership that are immediately allocated to the remaining owners if one owner dies.

Junk Bond: An investment with a higher default risk compared to higher quality bonds.

Liability: A debt owed to someone else, usually a financial institution; for example, a car loan, student loan or mortgage.

Liquid: A term that describes an asset that can be quickly converted to cash so that it can be used easily and immediately.

Loss: With respect to investing, a decrease in the value of an asset from its purchase price; with respect to insurance, when you no longer have something of value or it has been damaged.

Marketable Security: Any equity or debt investment that is readily salable.

Medicaid: A healthcare program for low-income families to pay for long-term medical and custodial care.

Medicare: A federal program providing health insurance to citizens age 65 and older.

Mortgage: A loan in which real estate is used as collateral.

Mutual Fund: A pool of funds collected from many people to buy stocks, bonds and other investments to meet the investors' objectives.

NASDAQ: A broad based index of more than 3,000 companies, many of which are in the technology industry.

Net Worth: The value of assets owned minus the amount of money owed.

Own Occupation Disability: Someone unable to perform the majority of duties for which they have been trained.

Passive Management: An investment style where a fund's portfolio mirrors a market index.

Pension: An employer-sponsored and funded retirement plan to provide retirement income to its workers.

Permanent Life Insurance: A policy that pays out upon the policyholder's death and accumulates value during the policyholder's lifetime.

Personal Financial Statement: A financial report that details an individual's income, expenses, assets and liabilities.

Personal Security Fund or Emergency Fund: An account in which you set aside money to be used for unexpected expenses.

Physical Asset: A tangible item of economic value; for example, art, real estate and equipment.

Pink Tax: The price difference between what women pay for female-specific products compared with gender-neutral goods or those marketed to men.

Portfolio: A strategic combination of investment assets; for example, stocks, bonds and cash.

Power of Attorney: The authority to act for another on financial, legal or medical affairs.

Premium: The amount of money paid for an insurance policy.

Prime Rate: The interest rate that commercial banks charge their most credit-worthy customers.

Prince Charming: A fairy tale character who comes to the rescue of a damsel in distress; also used as a term to refer to the idealized man some people dream of as a future spouse.

Profit: The money a business makes after accounting for all of its expenses.

Property and Casualty Insurance: Insurance that protects 1) the things you own and 2) you financially if someone sues you.

Queen: A female monarch or chieftain having supremacy in a specified realm.

Qualified Retirement Plan: A type of retirement plan established by a company for the benefit of its employees.

Rate of Return: The gain or loss on an investment over a specified period, expressed as a percentage of the investment's cost.

Renter's Insurance: Coverage that protects against losses to a tenant's personal property against losses resulting from liability claims.

Rule of 72: A shortcut to estimate the number of years required to double your money at a given annual rate of return.

Salary Deferral: An employee's election to set aside part of her current compensation to contribute to an employer-sponsored retirement.

Social Security Benefits: Monthly income paid to retired workers and their spouses who have paid into the system during their working years.

Sovereignty: Supreme power or authority.

S&P 500: American stock market index based on the value of 500 large public companies.

Spendthrift: Someone who spends money in an extravagant and irresponsible way.

Stockholder: Anyone who owns at least one share of a company's stock.

Target Date Fund: A mutual fund that automatically changes its asset mix according to a selected timeframe.

Tax-Deductible: An item or expense that can reduce a taxpayer's overall tax liability.

Tax-Deferred: Investment earnings such as interest, dividends or capital gains that accumulate tax free until the investor takes constructive receipt of them; aka, tax-sheltered.

Total Return: The sum of the income an investment generates along with the growth it provides.

Umbrella Insurance: An additional layer of coverage above the limits of traditional property and casualty insurance.

Universal Life Insurance: A permanent insurance policy that allows changes to the amount of the death benefit, premium amount and payment period; aka, adjustable life or flexible life.

Variable Expenses: Costs that may increase, decrease or remain the same.

Variable Rate: Loans or investments without a fixed rate of interest or return.

Wicked: Causing or likely to cause harm, trouble or distress to a damsel.

Will: A legal declaration of how a person's property or assets are to be distributed after death.

Yield: The income returned from holding an investment; for example, interest or dividends. It is expressed as an annual percentage rate based on the investment's value.

Appendix I

FINRA Quiz

Test your financial literacy to see how you compare to 25,000 Americans.

Q: Suppose you have $100 in a savings account earning 2% interest a year. After five years, how much would you have?

More than $102
Exactly $102
Less than $102
Don't know

A: You'll have **more than $102** at the end of five years because your interest will compound over time. In other words, you'll earn interest on the money you save and on the interest your savings earned in prior years. Here's how the math works: A savings account with $100 and a 2% annual interest rate would earn $2 in interest for an ending balance of $102 by the end of the first year. Applying the same 2% interest rate, the $102 would earn $2.04 in the second year for an ending balance of $104.04 at the end of that year. Continuing in this same pattern, the savings account would grow to $110.41 by the end of the fifth year.

Q: Imagine that the interest rate on your savings account is 1% a year and inflation is 2% a year. After one year, would the money in the account buy more, the same or less than it does today?

More
Same
Less
Don't know

A: You will have **less** because you have to factor in inflation. Inflation is the rate at which the price of goods and services rises. If the annual inflation rate is 2% but your savings account only earns 1%, the cost of goods and services has outpaced the buying power of the money in your savings account that year. Put another way, your buying power has not kept up with inflation.

Q: If interest rates rise, what will typically happen to bond prices? Will they rise, fall, stay the same or is there no relationship between the two?

Rise
Fall
Stay the same
No relationship
Don't Know

A: When interest rates rise, bond prices **fall**; and when interest rates fall, bond prices rise. This is because as interest rates go up, newer bonds come to market paying higher interest yields than older bonds already in the hands of investors, making the older bonds worth less.

Q: True or False: A 15-year mortgage typically requires higher monthly payments than a 30-year mortgage but the total interest over the life of the loan will be less.

True
False
Don't know

A: True. Assuming the same interest rate for both loans, you will pay less in interest over the life of a 15-year loan than you would with a 30-year loan because you repay the principal at a faster rate. This also explains why the monthly payment for a 15-year loan is higher. Let's say you get a 30-year mortgage at 6% on a $150,000 home. You will pay $899 a month in principal and interest charges. Over 30 years, you will pay $173,757 in interest alone, but a 15-year mortgage at the same rate will cost you less. You will pay $1,266 each month but only $77,841 in total interest — nearly $100,000 less.

Q: True or False: Buying a single company's stock usually provides a safer return than a stock mutual fund.

True
False
Don't know

A: False. In general, investing in a stock mutual fund is less risky than investing in a single stock because mutual funds offer a way to diversify. Diversification means spreading your risk by spreading your investments. With a single stock, all of your eggs are in one basket. If the price falls when you sell, you lose money. With a mutual fund that invests in the stocks of dozens (or even hundreds) of companies, you lower the chances that a price decline for any single stock will impact your return. Diversification generally results in a more consistent performance in different market conditions.

BONUS QUESTION: *Suppose you owe $1,000 on a loan and the interest rate you are charged is 20% per year compounded annually. If you didn't pay anything on the loan – neither principal nor interest – at this interest rate, how many years would it take for the amount you owe to double?*

Less than 2 years
2 to 4 years
5 to 9 years
10 or more years
Don't know

A: If you ignored interest compounding, borrowing at 20% per year would lead to doubling what you owe in five years. Someone who knows about "interest on interest" may select a number less than five as the answer. Someone who understands the "rule of 72" would know that it would be about 3.6 years, which makes the correct answer **2 to 4 years**. In finance, the rule of 72 is a method for estimating an investment's doubling time. The rule number (72) is divided by the interest percentage per period to obtain the approximate number of periods (usually years) required for doubling. The other responses reflect a misunderstanding of the concept of interest accrual.

Appendix II

Risk Tolerance Questionnaire

Circle the responses that best describe you. Remember that risk tolerance is largely subjective, so there are no right or wrong answers.

LIFE STAGE
1. What is your current age?
a) 65 or older.
b) 60 to 64.
c) 55 to 59.
d) 50 to 54.
e) Under 50.

2. When do you expect to need to withdraw cash from your investment portfolio?
a) In less than 1 year.
b) Within 1 to 2 years.
c) Within 2 to 5 years.
d) Within 5 to 10 years.
e) Not for at least 10 years.

FINANCIAL RESOURCES
3. How many months of current living expenses could you cover with your present savings and liquid short-term investments before you would have to draw on your investment portfolio?
a) Less than 3 months.
b) 3 to 6 months.
c) 6 to 12 months.
d) More than 12 months.

4. Over the next few years, what do you expect will happen to your income?
a) It will probably decrease substantially.
b) It will probably decrease slightly.
c) It will probably stay the same.
d) It will probably increase slightly.
e) It will probably increase substantially.

5. What percentage of your gross annual income have you been able to save in recent years?
a) None.
b) 1 to 5%.
c) 5 to 10%.
d) 10 to 15%.
e) More than 15%.

6. Over the next few years, what do you expect will happen to your rate of savings?
a) It will probably decrease substantially.
b) It will probably decrease slightly.
c) It will probably stay the same.
d) It will probably increase slightly.
e) It will probably increase substantially.

EMOTIONAL RISK TOLERANCE
7. What are your return expectations for your portfolio?
a) I don't care if my portfolio keeps pace with inflation; I just want to preserve my capital.
b) My return should keep pace with inflation, with minimum volatility.
c) My return should be slightly more than inflation, with only moderate volatility.
d) My return should significantly exceed inflation, even if this could mean significant volatility.

8. How would you characterize your personality?

a) I'm a pessimist. I always expect the worst.

b) I'm anxious. No matter what you say, I'll worry.

c) I'm cautious but open to new ideas. Convince me.

d) I'm objective. Show me the pros and cons and I can make a decision and live with it.

e) I'm optimistic. Things always work out in the end.

9. When monitoring your investments over time, what do you think you will tend to focus on?

a) Individual investments that are doing poorly.

b) Individual investments that are doing very well.

c) The recent results of my overall portfolio.

d) The long-term performance of my overall portfolio.

10. Suppose you had $10,000 to invest and the choice of five different portfolios with a range of possible outcomes after a single year. Which of the following portfolios would you feel most comfortable investing in?

a) Portfolio A, which could have a balance ranging from $9,900 to $10,300 at the end of the year.

b) Portfolio B, which could have a balance ranging from $9,800 to $10,600 at the end of the year.

c) Portfolio C, which could have a balance ranging from $9,600 to $11,000 at the end of the year.

d) Portfolio D, which could have a balance ranging from $9,200 to $12,200 at the end of the year.

e) Portfolio E, which could have a balance ranging from $8,400 to $14,000 at the end of the year.

11. If the value of your investment portfolio dropped by 20% in one year, what would you do?

a) Fire my investment advisor.

b) Move my money to more conservative investments immediately to reduce the potential for future losses.

c) Monitor the situation and if it looks like things could continue to deteriorate, move some of my money to more conservative investments.

d) Consult with my investment advisor to ensure that my asset allocation is correct, and then ride it out.

e) Consider investing more because prices are so low.

12. Which of the following risks or events do you fear most?

a) A loss of principal over any period of one year or less.

b) A rate of inflation that exceeds my rate of return over the long term, because it will erode the purchasing power of my money.

c) Portfolio performance that is insufficient to meet my goals.

d) Portfolio performance that is consistently less than industry benchmarks.

e) A missed investment opportunity that could have yielded higher returns over the long term, even though it entailed higher risk.

Scoring:

Give the following points for each answer: a = 1, b = 2, c = 3, d = 4, e = 5

Question Number	My Answer	Point Value
Life Stage Questions		
1		
2		
Life Stage Score (add results from 1 and 2)		
Financial Resources and Emotional Risk Tolerance Questions		
3		
4		
5		
6		
7		
8		
9		
10		
11		
12		
Investment Style Score (add results from 3 through 12)		

Interpretation of Results:

If your Life Stage Score is:	Then your Investment Time Horizon is:
1 to 3	Short-term (5 years or less)
4 to 6	Intermediate-term (5 to 10 years)
7 to 10	Long-term (over 10 years)
If your Investment Style Score is:	**Then Your Investment Style is:**
5 to 10	Very conservative
11 to 20	Moderately conservative
21 to 30	Moderate
31 to 40	Moderately Aggressive
41 to 50	Very aggressive

Source: The Canadian Institute of Financial Planners (CIFPs), an association of Canadian CFP™ licensees, Mississauga, Ontario, Canada. www.CIFPs.ca.

Appendix III

Life's Expenses

Food

Housing

    Mortgage or rent

    Real estate taxes (county and city)

    Utilities (gas, water, cable)

    Phone

    Other

Clothing

Health and Fitness

Auto (gas, insurance and maintenance)

Insurances (medical, dental, life and homeowner's)

Savings and Investments

Entertainment, Recreation and Vacations

Additional Resources

The following is a list of useful websites and other sources that any sovereign queen can access to help her financially plan for today, tomorrow and happily ever after.

BANKING and LENDING

- www.bankrate.com - Comparison shop for banks for both saving and borrowing. It has dozens of calculators to help you calculate the costs and benefits of different products and strategies.

BUDGETING

- www.americasaves.org - Tips and tools for savers young and old. Created by the nonprofit Consumer Federation of America, their tagline is "Start Small. Think Big."
- www.smartaboutmoney.org - Created by the nonprofit National Endowment for Financial Education, you can find worksheets, courses and quizzes regarding almost all of the topics in *It's Good to be Queen*.
- www.mint.com - Free and easy-to-use web-based personal finance software with budgeting, tracking and online bill paying.

CAREER PLANNING

- www.monster.com - Beyond just being a place to post your resume, its Career Resources pages are helpful to both the employed and jobseekers.
- www.indeed.com - The "Find Salaries" pages allow you to search

and compare salaries for different careers.

- https://womenandgoodjobs.org/women-middle-skill-jobs/ resources - Find links to apprenticeships, trade groups and professional organization for a wide variety of non-traditional occupations for women.

CHARITABLE GIVING

- www.charitynavigator.org - The place to start researching and evaluating your favorite charities. Search for charities that support causes near and dear to your heart.

CREDIT

- www.annualcreditreport.com - Request your free credit report every year to make sure it's correct and current. Read up on identity theft and how to protect yourself from being a victim.

EQUAL PAY

- http://www.huffingtonpost.com/jillian-berman/yes-by-any-way-you-measur_b_4725356.html - This Huffington Post blog post includes statistics on pay for women versus men.
- www.nwlc.org - Learn about the issues surrounding equal pay, including past history, present facts, and what you can do to make for a brighter future.

FINDING A FINANCIAL ADVISOR

- http://www.plannersearch.org - Hosted by the Financial Planning Association, search here for a certified financial planner in your area.
- https://brokercheck.finra.org - Research your financial advisor, her firm, her employment history, her licenses and any client complaints.

LIFE INSURANCE

- http://www.lifehappens.org/insurance-overview/life-insurance/calculate-your-needs - An easy-to-use calculator to determine how much life insurance you need based on your personal financial situation.

LONG-TERM CARE

- https://www.genworth.com/about-us/industry-expertise/cost-of-care.html - Illustrates the different types of care and their costs around the country.

NEGOTIATING SKILLS FOR WOMEN

- *Women Don't Ask* and *Ask For It,* both by Linda Babcock and Sara Leschever. These books are required reading for any woman seeking the motivation and skills to negotiate with confidence.
- https://tepper.cmu.edu/prospective-students/executive-education/leadership-for-women/leadership-and-negotiation-academy-for-women - If you've got the time and resources, attend the Tepper Women's Leadership and Negotiation Academy at Carnegie Mellon University. Taught by experts in the field, you'll join a group of like-minded women who will support you personally and professionally.

Acknowledgments

Many people supported me through the process of writing this book and deserve thanks:

Anne Hussman, Mary Richter and Joanna Williams.

My fellow shareholders in MD&A Financial Management Co., who have been great partners.

My network of professional women who support my mission and message, especially MJ Tocci and all involved with the Premier cohort of the CMU Negotiation Academy for Women.

The team that helped to make this book a book, especially Gina Mazza.

And all my other friends, family and colleagues who would have supported me had I the courage to share with them that I was writing a book.

It's Good to be Queen

About the Author

A CERTIFIED FINANCIAL PLANNER™ professional, Roselyn is passionate about helping women feel empowered financially. She is President of MD&A Financial Management Co. and a Registered Representative and Investment Advisory Associate of Berthel Fisher & Company Financial Services, Inc. Roselyn is a graduate of Bucknell University with an MBA from the University of Pittsburgh.

On the board of the Women & Girls Foundation, Roselyn actively supports other women professionals and woman-owned businesses. She has been a guest writer for the *Pittsburgh Post-Gazette* and *Pittsburgh Business Times,* and a guest on the radio program *Essential Pittsburgh.*

Roselyn resides in the South Hills of Pittsburgh, Pennsylvania with her husband, two sons and an adorable German Shepherd.

Learn more at Good2BQueen.com.